What Difference Does Difference Make?

What Difference Does Difference Make?

Teacher Reflections on Diversity, Literacy, and the Urban Primary School

Anne Haas Dyson
University of California, Berkeley

WITH

Andrea Bennett, *Oakland Unified School District*

Wanda Brooks, *University of California, Berkeley*

Judi Garcia, *Oakland Unified School District*

Carolyn Howard-McBride, *Oakland Unified School District*

Judy Malekzadeh, *Oakland Unified School District*

Carol Pancho, *Oakland Unified School District*

Linda Rogers, *Oakland Unified School District*

Louise Rosenkrantz, *Berkeley Unified School District*

Elizabeth Scarboro, *University of California, Berkeley*

Kristin Stringfield, *Berkeley Unified School District*

Jill Walker, *Oakland Unified School District*

Elise Yee, *Oakland Unified School District*

National Council of Teachers of English
1111 W. Kenyon Road, Urbana, Illinois 61801-1096

Editor: Peter Feely

Cover and Interior Design: Victoria Martin Pohlmann

NCTE Stock Number: 56576-3050

Library of Congress Cataloging-in-Publication Data

Dyson, Anne Haas.
     What difference does difference make? : teacher reflections on diversity, literacy, and the urban primary school / Anne Haas Dyson with Andrea Bennett . . . [et al.].
       p. cm.
     Includes bibliographical references (p.).
     ISBN 0-8141-5657-6 (pbk.)
     1. Education, Primary—California—Oakland. 2. Language arts teachers—California—Oakland. 3. Multicultural education—California—Oakland. 4. Language arts (Primary)—California—Oakland. I. Title.
LA245.O4D97 1997
372.24'1'0979466—dc20   96-23993
                                                                               CIP

Contents

Prologue

First-graders Roman (who was born in Germany) and Aaron (who was born in the United States) are sitting side-by-side coloring their maps of Mexico, a regular study topic in this once-Mexican land of California. As they work on their flags' eagles, they confirm each other's color choices: blue eyes? black feathers? a white streak maybe? Amidst their talk of color and country, it is not surprising, perhaps, that the conversation turns to their own colors and countries:

Roman: Aaron, are you African American?

Aaron: Yeah—NO!

Roman: What are you? American American?

Aaron: (with definiteness) I'm a *nice, young, man*. That's what I am.

And then, after a pause:

Aaron: (with irritation) WHAT ARE YOU, *PSYCH*? I'm a African American. What are you?

Roman: I'm a German American.

Aaron: Oh. But I wasn't born in Africa.

Roman and Aaron are, in one sense, very American kids. "In America," says the actor and playwright Anna Deveare Smith, "identity is always being negotiated" (1993, p. xxxiii). Our very Americanness, she suggests, is found in our struggle to find words to name the *I*, the *you*, the *we*. Our one nation "*is*," to add Geneva Smitherman's words, "a land of many voices; it *is* a nation of many cultures" (1990, p. 111). Our national identity is rooted in symbols like the Statue of Liberty, with its invitation to the many, and the Constitution, with its promised pluralism.

Nonetheless, as both Smith and Smitherman note—and Roman and Aaron illustrate—it *is* hard to talk about difference. There are tensions between our valued symbols and our historical record. These tensions provide complex overtones to any talk about difference, making such talk hard to interpret, even for the very young. "What are you, psych?" Aaron asks. Are you blind, confused, curious? Do you take me for a fool? I am, and I am not, what you say and you see. And, by the way, what are you?

In the midst of their efforts to make their coloring exactly alike, Aaron and Roman venture into the complexities of color, culture, and nation state. In so doing, the boys are themselves a symbol for what Celia Genishi calls (in Chapter 6 of this volume) the "yin-yang" of teaching: "the capacity to hold in mind apparently opposing ideas to form a workable whole," to understand how difference "'makes all the difference' at times and 'not much difference at all' at other times."

Like the boys, the language arts teachers whose voices appear herein are not blind to the differences that are so salient in our national life, especially differences of race, ethnicity, culture, language, and socioeconomic status. These differences, they know, influence both children's and adults' sense of social belonging and personhood, their sense of social possibility and constraint, and, moreover, the nature of their experiential and language resources. Thus, they gathered together to talk about the yin-yang of teaching, about the difference difference made in their everyday lives with young children.

The group's talk, reconstructed herein, is intended to stimulate, provoke, and invite talk in other places. After all, phenomena as complex as negotiating differences and the yin-yang of teaching are not easily captured in static words. They have to be experienced in the very struggle to find the right words. That *is* the American way, suggests Smith (1993, p. xii); the American character, she writes, is found, "not in what has been fully articulated, but in what is in the process of being articulated . . . in our struggle to be together in our differences" (another yin-yang response).

As teachers, our group was not, I hasten to add, naive. During the evening meeting in which we brainstormed discussion questions that might deepen readers' responses, one of us asked where this hoped-for talk would go on. I thought, perhaps, a faculty meeting.

"Have you been to a faculty meeting in [my school district] lately?" another of us asked.

And everyone laughed.

Making opportunities for professional reflection and collaborative growth a normal part of teachers' lives will, as we know, require widespread changes of institutional structure, professional vision, and public will. In the interest of such changes, we offer this illustration of professional reflection by teachers working in, for, and toward an American democracy. We offer our words. May they inspire many more.

Acknowledgments

As group instigator, I gained the company of teacher colleagues with the assistance of Alice Kawazoe, Director of Staff Development and Curriculum for Oakland Unified School District, and with the encouragement of other colleagues and friends, especially Elizabeth Simons, Mary K. Healy, and Celia Genishi. Patricia Lambert Stock, editor of *English Education,* provided much appreciated enthusiasm and much needed editorial expertise; with her help, a first version of our dialogues appeared in that journal in May 1995.

A project involving so many teachers, schools, and children would not have been possible without the financial assistance of the Spencer Foundation. Additional support was provided by the Educational Research and Development Center Program (grant number R117G10036), U.S. Department of Education, and by the Oakland Unified School District. The findings and opinions expressed herein, however, are those of the group participants, not those of the Spencer Foundation, the U.S. Department of Education, or the Oakland Schools.

This project also benefitted from the involvement of graduate students from the University of California at Berkeley. Among these students were group participants Elizabeth Scarboro and Wanda Brooks, who attended group meetings and joined me in visiting schools and who also managed correspondence, phone calls, transcriptions, photocopying, and on and on. In the closing months of this project, I was greatly assisted by Gwen Larsen and Sheila Shea, who reviewed and reproofed this book, in addition to continuing the managerial work Elizabeth and Wanda had begun. Throughout the project, Steve Kang was a terrific photographer.

Finally, I would like to acknowledge two group members who were not able to regularly attend our meetings: Marty Conrad, of Berkeley Unified, and Verna Henderson, of Oakland Unified.

A warm thanks to all.

Chapter **1** | Teaching in City Schools

In order to live in the city, I needed to ally myself, in some concrete, practical, if limited way, with the possibilities. So I went up to Convent Avenue and 133rd Street and was interviewed for a teaching job....

A. Rich, "Teaching Language in Open Admissions"

It is late afternoon on a Tuesday, the day the teachers "meet for tea," as Elise, one of us, says. From downtown Oakland, with its commercial businesses and restaurants, from East Oakland with its railroad tracks and industrial plants, and from the greener, tree-lined streets on the Oakland/Berkeley border, ten (plus or minus one) teachers are finding their way out of classrooms and conversations, pressing obligations and minor distractions. The schools they are leaving serve children of diverse cultural and linguistic heritage, of different economic circumstance and familial situation.

It is, in fact, those differences that the teachers have in common. That is, the teachers all identify, in one way or another, with the urban complexity of the East San Francisco Bay. Indeed, some of the teachers have deep roots here. Elise, for example, is teaching at the very school she attended as a child, and Carolyn and Andrea are also graduates of the Oakland public schools. *All* of the teachers, however, have professional histories shaped by the changing demographics and politics of urban schools.

During their teaching careers, which average about twenty years, some schools populated primarily by African American or Latino children have been transformed as new immigrant populations have entered the city; other schools have become "grandma" schools, serving not neighborhood children, but the grandchildren of neighborhood elders who care for those children. And, as in cities all over the country, some schools are in neighborhoods that have lost their economic footing, places where both parents and teachers worry about children's safety. As budgets have been scrunched, integration policies changed, regulations for bilingual programs rewritten, and requirements for compensatory education funds transformed, the teachers have had their positions shifted, their colleagues transferred, their students redistributed.

Still, these are teachers who seem to feel a need to be in the thick of things, as it were, and, like Adrienne Rich in the opening quote, to ally themselves with possibilities, to make a positive difference in the changing version of America taking shape around them. And it is the desire to reflect upon sociocultural differences and the work of teaching, particularly teaching the language arts, that is bringing the teachers to the university for "tea," although some say it's the table filled with snacks, the cushy chairs, the open windows on a tree-shaded campus—a peaceful place (aside from the tension of finding a parking place). So this Tuesday, like others, we will interweave talk about young children's language and literacy with broader issues of teaching and diversity.

This document is, in the main, the report of our Tuesday teas, supplemented with observations and audiotaped records made in the teachers' schools by the university members of the group—Elizabeth Scarboro and Wanda Brooks, two young teachers and graduate students, and me. It is an examination, from the teachers' perspectives, of sociocultural diversity and teaching. And it is the focus on teachers' perspectives that makes this document relatively unique.

Teaching amidst sociocultural diversity is a matter of great current concern in preservice education and staff development. Teachers, it is argued, need to be more adequately prepared to teach children in urban schools (e.g., Darling-Hammond, 1993; Ladson-Billings, 1994; Sleeter, 1993; Smitherman, 1986). In writing pedagogy in particular, many educators have written of the need to examine pedagogical practices and the ways in which they may not exploit the language and experiential resources of our diverse population (e.g., Bartolomé, 1994; Delpit, 1988; Dyson, 1993; Gutierrez, 1993; Reyes, 1992; Scott, 1990).

On the other hand, it is *also* argued that, in this work of rethinking pedagogical practice and, more broadly, urban teaching, experienced teachers are an untapped resource (e.g., Connell, 1994; Genishi, 1992; Montero-Sieburth, 1989). As Montero-Sieburth (1989, p. 336) argues, urban school teachers often "have to live down" media presentations of negative images of city schools and, indeed, of their students. And yet, experienced teachers have much accumulated knowledge as the "frontline workers" (Connell, 1994, p. 138), the "cultural brokers" (Heath, 1983, p. 369), the "mediators" of all who have "a stake in literacy education—teachers, parents, children, administrators, politicians, textbook publishers, and the press" (Florio-Ruane, 1991, p. 252).

In order to make explicit some of this accumulated knowledge, we gathered every other week during the 1993–94 school year to reflect on our collective teaching experiences and, more particularly, to ask, in effect, what difference does "difference" make in our experience of the daily work of teaching? Our group was formed with the assistance of Alice Kawazoe, Director of Staff Development for Oakland Unified, who helped recruit a multiethnic group of experienced teachers, who were themselves working with children from diverse sociocultural backgrounds.

Our curricular focus was the teaching of writing, one common interest of group members—not surprising, perhaps, given the availability of professional development in writing curriculum through the National Writing Project, which took root in the Bay Area. Over time, our discussions of difference and child literacy broadened, became deeper, as we became more comfortable with each other and with the topic of difference itself. Our initial question evolved into more specific ones:

❖ What do we mean by "difference"?

❖ Who decides what or who is "different"?

❖ How and when do we experience "differences" in the course of our daily teaching? Are there particular dimensions of classroom life in which differences become salient in positive or problematic ways? What makes them "positive" or "problematic"?

❖ How do we make literacy curricula open to children's diverse experiences and resources? How do we keep our activities flexible and our expectations forward looking?

❖ How do we help children themselves live in a world of differences?

Our intention is to offer a framework for teacher reflection, a framework grounded in our own reflections on classroom experiences and one that will help other teachers of young children respond to the complexities of human learning. In this opening chapter we address the overriding issues of difference that interweave all the chapters to come, then briefly explain the procedures through which we explored differences, and, finally, introduce our group in action, presenting segments of group discussions that illustrate our collective feelings about the challenges and rewards of urban teaching.

My voice dominates this opening chapter more so than in the others. It was my desire for a study group, for colleagues with whom to explore common concerns about childhood, diversity, and literacy, that initiated the formation of the group. But, as is always the case in collaboration, the project took on a life of its own, and the "we" of the document is the collective, but not uniform, voice of a group of educators exploring the dramas (and comedies) of urban teaching.

In many ways, such teaching is not a distinctive breed, and our perspectives, we hope, will be of wide interest to teachers in diverse settings. But urban schools *are* sites in which teachers' mediating role is boldly outlined. Common instructional cliches—building on what children know, creating a community of learners, educating for democracy—assume new complexities. The always present gaps between the life-space of adults and children, between the authority and the governed, the teacher and the student, often are complicated by social, cultural, and linguistic gaps, among other possible differences. The need for teacher flexibility and imagination—and for schools that allow teachers negotiating power, as it were—are all writ large, as is, of course, the potential of teachers to ally themselves with the rich possibilities of the young.

On the Meaning of Difference: Identifying Who and What Is "Different"

"I talked to a teacher the other day who did a lesson on language," said Andrea one night, a lesson on vocabulary related to Halloween. That teacher "was very upset that the students did not know about Halloween. He emphasized that the students need to know the language that's the norm. So I asked him, 'Who sets the norm?' He always says that the students don't have certain things so they'll never be able to learn to read."

Andrea's comments make clear one of the difficulties we face in trying to make sense of difference: "Who sets the norm?" Who decides who and what is "different"? Issues of difference are related to the issues of power institutionalized in the school itself—which is one reason those issues are so very hard to talk about (Gillmore, Goldman, McDermott, & Smith, 1993). The school's grade-level designations, its observational checklists and evaluation tools, its report cards and its homework policies are all predicated on assumptions about the meaning of "readiness," of "literacy," of a "caring" parent and a "respectful" child.

As many educational anthropologists and sociologists have argued for at least three decades (e.g., see review, Cazden & Mehan, 1989), these assumptions are tied to the lifestyle of the powerful segment of our society, glossed by the word "mainstream" (meaning white and middle class). This fixing of the "norm" yields a tension-filled relationship with those families and children not included in that gloss: the school can be a foreign, alienating, disrespectful place where nobody seems to "care," a common complaint of working-class parents (Connell, 1994);

on the other hand, it is a critical avenue to desired knowledge and skills. The educational literature reflects this tension, sometimes highlighting concerns about nonmainstream students' access to that knowledge on the one hand (e.g., Delpit, 1988), sometimes questioning assumptions about what constitutes "access" and "knowledge" on the other (Perry & Fraser, 1993).

A focus on institutional assumptions helps explain who and what emerges as "different" in the course of everyday life at school. After all, every child is different, as is every classroom of children. For example, the teachers in our group often opened a story with a variant of the phrase, "Well *last* year's class . . . but *this* year's class. . . ." Indeed, a commonly identified tension in the life of the elementary school teacher is that between the individual and the group (e.g., Cortazzi, 1993; Jackson, 1990). But institutional assumptions about "normality" can reverberate among the children in our classes, highlighting children's cultural heritage, their ethnicity or race, language or dialect, and economic circumstance in ways that are problematic or productive—it all depends (Erickson, 1987). It is "what" it depends on that is the focus of this document.

For example, in one meeting, Louise talked about her kindergartner Tatanka, an American Indian child. Tatanka had had a difficult time adjusting to school and then, after just two weeks, he disappeared, apparently because of family custody disputes. He came back to the school a few months later, but not as "Tatanka"—as "Nathan." The teachers at his reservation school had changed his name.

Louise: They told him it wouldn't be a good name for him when he went out into the real community.

Anne: Who told him this?

Louise: His teacher. His teacher also told him (pause)

Andrea: That's a weird name?

Jill: Not an American name?

Louise: Right. I mean, in my class Tatanka is not a weird name.

Andrea: Right.

Soon, a complex discussion began, grounded in stories of children whose names had been changed by teachers or ridiculed by peers, about family members who had changed names mangled by English speakers or associated with English obscenities, stories of young children who could not answer the simple question "And what's your name?" because that name had been changed the night before by parents anxious for their child to fit in. Given the centrality of names, not only to establishing human connections, but also to early primary literacy curricula, something as simple as a child's name reverberates in surprisingly complex ways through the everyday experience of schooling. The discussion then was not so much about Tatanka, but about the complexities of difference, in this case cultural and linguistic, and the way that difference figures into school as institution, as negotiated human relationships, as a place for organized learning.

This concern with the way in which difference emerges in these three interrelated dimensions of school life—institutional structure, negotiated relationships, and instructional activities—took shape in the course of our Tuesday teas, as I explain in the following section.

Enacting the Teachers' Tea

Words like "difference" and "literacy" are abstract, slippery words that only gain meaning in the context of particular classrooms, activities, and participants. So, in our early meetings (the first two months), we talked about participants' classrooms and children, gaining some insight into the variation in situations that we collectively included. And we also talked in detail about literacy curricula, identifying instructional contexts we had in common: all of the teachers, for example, had a regular writing time, in which the children did "free choice" writing and/or dictating in a journal, and everyone had some kind of sharing time, in which individual children could present their writing.

During the next six months the teachers took turns presenting case studies of children from their classrooms, choosing children who in some way evidenced the particular sociocultural resources of the communities served by their schools. For these cases, the teachers gave general introductions to each child (e.g., child's age, ethnicity, language(s), friends, temperament), and then they gave specific information about how the child participated in the literacy activities—especially the writing activities—the group had in common.

For example, teachers talked about (1) who children interacted with during writing, (2) the themes, discourse structures, and languages that figured into children's writing, (3) the responses children valued from—or offered—others about texts, and (4) any evident links between children's texts and their in-school relationships and their out-of-school lives. The teachers also talked about (5) their own relationships with children's families and, at times, with other teachers who worked with (or had worked with) the children. This talk about individual children yielded the project data—transcriptions of our meetings, all of which were audiotaped.

During this period of case-study presentation, Elizabeth, Wanda, and I began visiting the teachers' classrooms, meeting their children and, in particular, the case study or "focal" children. These visits helped establish a working relationship with the teachers: we had seen their schools, their playgrounds, their classrooms, their children. The teachers were also encouraged to visit each other. In the last months of the school year we collected audiotapes of all case-study children's interactions with teachers and peers and, in addition, photographs of each classroom.

All group members engaged in ongoing analytic discussion of the presented cases. In effect, the teachers presented their constructions of children's actions and their own responses to those actions—descriptions that revealed their understandings of the practice of literacy teaching as articulated in the day-to-day experiences with children. As chair of the teacher meetings, I used the transcripts of our meetings to prepare summaries of our analytic discussions for elaboration and refinement by the teachers and also to re-present case-study material for more focused discussions of important points.

It was through this joint analysis of commonalities and differences in our constructions or narratives of everyday teaching that we formulated our understandings of what difference difference makes, that is, of the kinds of variation in child language and cultural resources that become salient in literacy instruction and, more broadly, the nature of flexible adaption to not only the children but also to administrators, parents, and colleagues in the complex environment of urban schools. Thus, as in other teacher study groups, our perspectives on teaching and learning were shaped by the presentation and ongoing analysis of teachers' experiences (Cochran-Smith & Lytle, 1993; Genishi, 1992).

From the analysis of our meetings, we have developed a set of nested themes that present teaching as a matter of responding to children within the day-to-day enactment of classroom activities and, at the same time, that place those moments within the larger contexts of the classroom community and the school as an institution. Thus, our approach to teaching and learning is compatible with contextual and interactional perspectives on classroom life developed by educational anthropologists and sociolinguists (e.g., Cazden, 1988; Erickson, 1986; Florio-Ruane, 1989; Jacob & Jordan, 1993). Teaching is something that happens as people interact with each other; the quality of that teaching depends upon and supports the quality of human relations, not only in each classroom, but in the larger structure of the school as a whole.

The group as a whole worked to identify segments of discussions and classroom observations that illustrate most clearly our framework—our set of nested themes. As group chair and editor, I have woven these illustrations together in the chapters to follow; other group participants have responded to drafts—commenting, revising, or elaborating as they so chose. In this document, then, we discuss teachers' interactions with individual children in the context of the school and the school district as institutional structures, in the community of the classroom, and in the immediate context of particular classroom activities. And throughout, we consider how these interactions are informed by issues of "difference."

We emphasize the ways in which sociocultural differences are highlighted in school life because we are sensitive to the complexity of interrelated differences that may or may not become relevant in the course of our daily interactions with individual children. Among these differences are not only those of economic class, language, and cultural background tied to ethnic or racial heritage, but also those of physical abilities and demeanor, age and age-related culture, and on and on. Indeed, it is this complexity of differences that may make it hard to understand where children are coming from, so to speak, in any one teaching moment. In O'Loughlin's words:

> Each student possesses multiple frames of reference with which to construct knowledge by virtue of their ethnic background, race, class, gender, language usage, religious, cultural, and political identities.... The potential for knowledge construction depends very much on how schools react to students' attempts to employ these diverse frameworks for meaning-making. (1992, p. 5)

Thus, we worried both about stereotyping children—reducing complex individuals to simplistic examples of one kind of difference—and about being ignorant of the particular home cultures and socioeconomic circumstances of the particular children in each school.

Further, we avoid simple prescriptions for practice. Again, exactly what and how differences figure into teaching and learning depends, in part, on the particularities of each school population. For example, both Judi and Judy were bilingual teachers. However, Judy's class consisted entirely of children of Mexican heritage; the children were learning literacy primarily in Spanish, although they read and wrote English as well. On the other hand, Judi's children were of diverse backgrounds; while her school is known as a Spanish bilingual school, only half of Judi's children spoke Spanish. For Judi, then, language was a relatively greater curricular challenge, and her narratives reflected her emphasis on children's use of different languages.

Further, the identification of differences as problems or possibilities also depends on the institutional characteristics of each school, its ways of organizing time and space, of distributing resources to teachers, teachers to children, and of evaluating the efforts of both (e.g., Florio-Ruane, 1989; Leacock, 1969; Lightfoot, 1978). To elaborate, there are many *horizontal* differences among children (e.g., differences of language, cultural style, familial circumstance, or other "differences that shouldn't mean one person is any better than another," as Carolyn said). But such sociocultural and linguistic differences can be institutionally framed as correlates of academic deficiencies, from the very start of a child's school life. "Kindergarten checklists" and grade-level achievement tests traditionally monitor *vertical* differences among children (i.e., differences in where children fall on the very narrow band of abilities and skills that mark even young children as "smart" or "not," "ready" or "not," "at risk" or "not").

FIGURE 1 | JUDI'S CHILDREN ALL READY FOR RECESS.

Children who come to school already knowing and able to display on demand these sorts of knowledge help ease the pressure of regulated environments, environments which may seem better suited to "robots" than children (as Carolyn also said). For example, Louise's kindergartner Faye was a thoughtful, self-reflective observer, a lover of literature and of words, a superb storyteller who drew on the verbal traditions of her African American heritage, *and* a child who was beginning to learn sound/symbol connections. But institutional definitions of competent youngsters "ready" for first grade have increasingly focused on narrow literacy skills (e.g., letter names and sounds), a focus that has contributed to the dramatic increase in "unready" children of nonmainstream cultural and linguistic backgrounds, children labeled as academic failures at the tender ages of five and six (Shepard, 1991).

All group members were involved in exploring alternative assessments at the district, school, or classroom level; still, given present institutional constraints, it can be hard to be "patient," in Louise's words, "to really let Faye use all of her verbal skills and all of her excitement" and not get "*so* stuck with her on sound/symbol [and] how are you going to be on the CTBS [the California Test of Basic Skills]." As will be evident in the discussions ahead, all of the teachers worked hard to make visible children's competence and to acknowledge the breadth of language, symbolic, and problem-posing and -solving skills needed in our world—without abandoning the need to straightforwardly help children learn traditional school knowledge and skills.

Through this document, the result of our teacher teas, we hope to support other teachers' reflections on their own teaching lives, on the ways in which difference figures as problem or resource in—or, conversely, as a taken-for-granted aspect of—the everyday work of teaching. Below, I bring readers into our teas, presenting more fully our group's feelings about the challenges and the rewards of urban teaching.

Ambivalence and Its Antidote: Community Connection, Personal Responsibility, and Collegial Support

One Tuesday, the teachers' talk turned to a recent piece in a Bay Area weekly newspaper, a piece that was startlingly critical about a local elementary school. The people in our group generally felt good about their schools; indeed, some, like Judi, talked about their schools in affectionate ways, as exciting places with innovative programs and, most importantly, as places that were warmly supportive of faculty and children. Still, the teachers also were no strangers to the sorts of problems the article discussed—although the severity of the problems was both breathtaking and maddening.

The school, said the paper, was filled with tensions between and among administrators, parents, teachers, and kids. The school's children came from an economically hard-pressed section of the city, one with problems of youth gangs and drug violence. Moreover, the children lived in racially separated neighborhoods (African American, Latino, and Southeast Asian), and they were segregated once again in the school, as poorly administered instructional programs splintered the children and the staff as well, or so reported the article. The children were integrated only on the playground, where fights were common, aggravated perhaps by the lack of anything to do out on the asphalt; play equipment was "off limits," wrapped in yellow tape since the death of a child on another playground revealed the limited protection afforded young heads and limbs by shredded, worn padding. In the classroom, the main effort was to keep the children in their seats, quiet, and, if possible, occupied.

Elise had brought copies of the article, and, as they were passed around, the discussion turned to the experience of being at such a school, where trust and faith in teachers and children seems at a minimum, where dispirited, overwhelmed administrators and teachers seem at a maximum, and where new teachers are left to flounder. Such schools exist, but they do not have to. As Louise said, after stories of despair and hope had been traded:

Louise: It is really school by school.

Carol: It is.

Judi: Yes, like *my* school. People are clamoring to work at my school even though we are just a bunch of portables stacked together, the bathrooms are a mess, and there is no teachers' room.

Louise: People want to be there because of what goes on.

Judi: Well, because of what goes on, and because there is a real good feeling on the staff.

FIGURE 2 | A SYMBOL OF FINANCIAL HARD TIMES: UNSAFE PLAYGROUND EQUIPMENT.

Judi then talks about her feeling upon walking into Andrea and Linda's school a few years earlier, a school also serving troubled neighborhoods but a school then in its heyday:

Judi: It is true that sometimes you walk in and you sense it right away. . . . I know that when I visited [Andrea and Linda's] school . . . it had posters all over [about teacher decision-making meetings]. There was really an excitement there. You really felt the support of the parents. You saw kids getting there on time, and you didn't see kids wandering a lot in the halls. Other schools, you can just sense this chaos—

a chaos more common when parents feel alienated from the school and powerless to intervene, said Andrea; when administrators are disrespectful of teachers, teachers of children, added Carolyn; and when everyone is ignorant of "the whole child" and the community being served, including the potential problems of economically depressed areas, reiterated Linda:

Linda: You have a bunch of children whose basic needs aren't being met. They don't feel safe. They may be hungry, and maybe they didn't sleep last night because their house was up all night. . . . But you are one on twenty-seven kids who need all your attention. . . . There are children having children, grandparents raising children, foster families, transitional children, homelessness, all of those things. . . . A new teacher will not continue teaching if she is not given major support.

Carolyn agreed with Linda's concerns and then elaborated:

Carolyn: But I can add that the families that you are describing, no matter what they are doing, ultimately, I have not had a parent yet that comes in and says, "I don't care if my child comes to school. I don't care if my child learns or not." . . . I play on that in my own classroom, and sometimes I have to go outside of my way to get [in touch with parents]. . . . So you need to have [new teachers] who can come in . . . and see how professionals who have been doing it for a long time, how they handle certain situations. I think that even people who have been doing it for a long time if you have been working in a "hills" school [in the affluent part of the city] and not a "flatlands" school perhaps that teacher may need to have an opportunity to see how that school *can* work.

Andrea's wry humor made this point clear:

Andrea: We had a teacher who was at our school who couldn't hang, and I took her class. . . . They sent her to a hills school, and I said, "Why does she get to go . . . and I have to stay here?" (laughs, as does the group). . . . Everybody was saying that. A brand new teacher who couldn't hang and they sent her up there. She is up there, and she is doing a beautiful job. . . . She went from a flatland school to a hills school, which is a totally different environment. . . ."

Still, these were teachers who, as Judi said, "all teach in the 'flatlands' schools . . . and we teach there by choice." Our discussions suggested three particularly strong reasons for this choice.

First, the teachers felt a sense of connection with their children and their communities. Some were teaching in schools in neighborhoods within which they had once lived; they had a sense of knowing the culture, of being a role model.

Elise, for example, talked about the changing nature of the Chinatown neighborhoods served by her school; she told us about neighborhood resources on Asian American cultures and brought samples of culturally informed materials developed at her school (not to mention tempting contributions to our snack supply). Elise and her kindergartners were hosts to Kristin's third graders, who took rapid transit from their Berkeley school for an afternoon visit.

To further illustrate, Andrea, who is African American, talked about the rewards of being a role model, someone in whom children could see themselves and their futures. In her words,

Andrea: Sometimes kids do need someone of their same race to bond with them . . . so that they can see that there is some hope for them. I can remember . . . a third grade student of mine, and I'm her godmother now, and she's 26. She stuck with me . . . all the way through her life and my life. She had her baby and she brought her baby to me, and told me I'm a grandmother now. . . . And she told me, "I always wanted to be like you. I waited to get married like you. I had my baby after I was married like you did. I went to college like you did. I want to be a teacher like you." She told me the other day, "Now I want a car like yours." (We all laugh.) . . . It's a really good feeling to talk to her and think, "This was my student. This was not a relative."

Other teachers too talked about personal experiences that engendered a sense of connection, of familiarity and comfort, with the children and families served by their schools. For example, Judi, who is European American, has been married for almost twenty-five years to her husband, who is of Mexican heritage. Jill, also European American, has had a lifelong interest in and comfort with diverse cultures, including her many years as a teacher of deaf persons. And all the teachers enjoyed the potential cultural richness of urban schools and, thus, the potential cultural richness of the classroom community when that diversity is exploited. "We got a lot of different cultures writing" here, "students [with] their own way of writing English," to use the words of the student editors of Judi's school literary magazine.

Moreover, the teachers also felt appreciated by parents. As Linda said, "I like the relationship with the children and the parents, and I think they're more appreciative" of school activities and programs than more affluent parents whose kids may have "been there, done that," to use Jill's words.

Second, the teachers in our group also felt some sense of agency, of ability to make a difference in their classrooms. We viewed the classroom as a "home away from home," as Carolyn said, and a place where the curriculum drew kids into that home and was "as much fun and as interesting" as we could make it, Louise added. Sometimes our very grammar revealed that this was not necessarily an easy thing to do. "I don't know why they—I don't know what *I* should do" in a particular situation, we would say.

This struggle could also be revealed in our group dynamics: one person worries about the relevance of education amidst neighborhood troubles, and someone else counters that "all parents care," that curricula can make a difference; at the next meeting, the same points are made, but the worrier and the classroom activist reverse roles. As a group, we were not of a single mind on all issues, but neither were we as individuals. "It all depends," could be our group motto, and "figuring out the human and situational complexities undergirding teaching decisions" one group aim.

Teaching anywhere, of course, can be an emotionally taxing experience, and a problem-solving, classroom-focused stance helps one keep going. Andrea's story about finding her student intern standing outside the school building, crying, struck a sympathetic chord with us all:

Andrea: I said, "What happened?" These are *first* graders. She said, "My lesson was a flop." She's standing out there, and she's trying to get herself together so she can go back into the room. . . . Now it's funny, but then it was sad. So I talked to her and said, "You cannot just give up. Just change your lesson. Do something else." So she went back in and she tried again. And after a while she began to catch on and do OK.

There was a small chorus of voices saying, in effect, "I still go home and cry."

Andrea: Right. I go home and say, "Tomorrow I'm going to do this. I'm going to change this. It didn't work." Eleanor, that was her name. She was another one who stood there crying. . . .

Teacher agency was linked to child agency. Over and over again, when teachers felt frustrated or confused, they talked about paying attention to the children, trying to figure out another tack they might take, and sometimes directly asking the children for their help. Carol, for example, talked about a "really really difficult" class she had of almost all boys. Influenced by the professional discussions about Milwaukee's experimentation with all-male black schools, she wondered "how could I shape their environment so it meets their needs for a change?" So she designed classroom activities, including a survey, to figure out the children's own views on what made it hard or easy to learn. "I wanted to see what kind of environment I could create using their feedback to kind of make it work for them."

Both community respect and personal agency are enacted and furthered through the sort of interaction we valued in the classroom, as Jill said the evening we discussed the news article:

Jill: It does sound bleak. I'm thinking of our own school, and we have a lot of similar problems. . . . But I do think, I realized since I was frustrated with all the problems that were going on . . . that I really needed to focus on my classroom. . . . I've worked really hard, all of us together in the classroom have worked really hard to create an environment where each of us does have a voice and they feel that whatever they have to say is very important. . . . And I really feel they start to value one another and we can work on the problems that we encompass in our own room, even though it's harder to work with them [the problems] outside the classroom.

A third and final reason for teacher satisfaction or its lack, for teaching as a source of satisfaction or aggravation, was the quality of interaction with colleagues. That is, the teachers in our group valued a dynamic *school* culture, a sense that each teacher's voice also mattered in the community of the school as a whole, that each was supporting as well as being supported by colleagues.

For example, Judy, an experienced teacher, said her comfort at her current school had to do with "feeling a part of the school. . . . There's so much going on here at [my school] that they need everyone to take a little part." Kristin, who was new to primary grade teaching, felt isolated at her current school, lonely for grade-level colleagues with whom to exchange curricular philosophies and daily plans, even for someone to eat lunch with: "I would go and hang out in the office so I could have some adult contact, y'know. I talked to the secretary, and I'd have to try to think of things to keep me in there."

A feeling of collegiality, most teachers felt, was related to the joint efforts of administrative leaders and active teachers on behalf of the school's children. Teachers must feel, as Judy said, that "the whole school is—all the children are my children." This feeling is not so easy at an inner-city school, where funds are limited, and federal, state, and local grants and regulations are targeted to specific needs and specific segments of a population (e.g., bilingual programs for diverse languages, compensatory education, Sheltered English classes).

Still, in the main, these were teachers who had found collegiality at some point in their careers, who knew what it felt like to be involved, supported, and interconnected with each other, with the community, and, most importantly, with the children. They wanted a voice that mattered, to be, in Judi's words, "making a difference whatever difference difference makes."

Our discussions of individual children consistently revealed these larger concerns about individual agency in the community of the classroom and of the school. To give a small example, a preview of a sort, one evening Carolyn presented the case of Darian, a first grader who had made great progress in literacy, including in learning to write. Indeed, when Carolyn told Darian she was going to be talking about his work at her teachers' meeting, Darian gave her some advice: "You should tell them that at first I didn't get it. . . . Then I got it. So that's why I can write this now." And what he could write included expressive statements that captured his conversational voice, his oral language, in a confident written one: "Football is my thing," began one of his pieces.

Carolyn's narrative about Darian's confident writing—and his admonition to his teacher—reflects not only Carolyn's valuing of *oral* resources and child experiences but also the kind of relationships Carolyn valued in her room. These were relationships in which children could and did speak up to teacher and peers. Moreover, in presenting Darian's case, Carolyn placed Darian's "getting it" in the context of her own efforts to ease children's paths between home and school, to help parents feel welcomed but not burdened, efforts she felt could be better supported by institutional structures.

In the chapters of this document we approach our multiple levels of interest in reverse order. We ask: When and how, in the course of teachers' experiences, do differences reveal institutional flexibility or rigidity, classroom cultural richness or sociocultural tension, permeable activities or impervious ones—in which children's language and experiences seem stymied, unengaged, or undirected? In Chapter 2 we address the institutional context of teaching and the ways in which it mediates relationships with parents, colleagues, and children; and then, in Chapter 3, we focus on teacher and peer relationships within the classroom community itself, including how children themselves address issues of difference. Chapter 4 centers on writing activities, considering the ways in which they are adapted for and made permeable to a diversity of child resources and needs. In each of these chapters, we introduce key themes— the ways in which differences become salient in our teaching experience—through presentation of particularly illustrative stories and transcript excerpts from our Tuesday teas; and we conclude each with a set of questions for teacher reflection and a sample of professional resources.

To bring together these multiple levels and to illustrate their interrelatedness, in Chapter 5 we present three portraits of children, based on their teachers' original oral presentations. Finally, in Chapter 6, we hear from educators based outside the classroom: Celia Genishi, Jerrie Cobb Scott, and Alice Kawazoe extend our dialogue into their own professional conversations about sociocultural diversity and teaching.

In the following chapter, then, we take you farther into our schools and classrooms through our narratives of teaching and of children learning, our stories about what difference difference makes.

Chapter **2** | Relationships in and out of the Classroom

"Who Am I to Them?"

> I loved my children and worked hard for them, lay awake at night worrying about them,
> spent my Sundays making word cards, tape recording stories for them to listen to,
> planning the week ahead. My back ached as I pinned their paintings to the wall, wrote
> the labels with a felt-tip pen, a good round hand, knowing even then the irony with
> which I would recall in later years the beacon light of the martyr's classroom shining into
> the winter's evening, the cleaner's broom moving through the corridor of the deserted
> schoolhouse.
>
> **C. Steedman,** *Past Tenses*

Writing about her experiences as an urban teacher, historian
Carolyn Steedman captures the way in which children occupy our imaginations and our time. Moreover, we too referred to the potential isolation of the teacher, institutionally slotted into her own room, responsible for her "own" children, a kind of "martyr" behind closed doors. Still, many of us have little opportunity to work in the peace of abandoned rooms, against the rhythm of "the cleaner's broom." Most important, we have no desire to be martyrs, and we see our satisfaction, indeed, our happiness, as teachers—and our ability to exploit the resources of our children—as dependent upon relationships with other adults.

In fact, in our very first discussions about diversity and *children,* varied *adults* made their appearance. When Andrea introduced herself, for example, she described her students as those often deemed ungovernable by other teachers. Judy talked about how intertwined her teaching day was with that of her colleagues, how they shared children of different ages and different language proficiencies. Linda talked about her desire to use familiar words from her kindergartners' physical surroundings to introduce them to school literacy, to show them that they *could* read—and she also talked about pressure from colleagues who expected not environmental print like *McDonald's* but "the letter of the week."

Other teachers, in fact, were our most consistent source of support and, also, of tension—it all depended. And what it depended on, in part, was how successfully we were able to overcome institutional separation, those closed classroom doors, and foster a sense of joint responsibility and mutual respect. Such a sense was dramatically lacking in a story Andrea told one evening about the troubled school discussed in the newspaper (a school in which she had once worked):

Andrea: There was a sub there, a young girl just out of college. And she said, "I cannot stand it" and walked out the door in the middle of class. She was *gone.* The kids were screaming and hollering. Then they called me to go over and take the class because "we have no one to take the class. . . ." So I go in there, and I am like, "What am I going to do? Who am I to them?"

"Who am I to them?" indeed. Underlying many of our discussions was a desire for the sort of urban schools described by Lightfoot (1978, p. 202), schools where children "belonged" to all the teachers, where they could "embrace" the entire building. Moreover, we desired space and time for the sort of collegial interaction that keeps institutional structures flexible, that both fosters and is fostered by a sense of connection that extends beyond the classroom to the school and, indeed, to the community.

In the sections below, then, we ask: What aspects of our teaching experiences suggest institutional flexibility or rigidity, opportunities lost or gained, to jointly meet the needs and exploit the resources of our diverse students? Which aspects influence whether or not vertical and horizontal differences become problems or resources, part of the expected texture of a school community or disruptions in the smooth operation of institutional life? In answer to these questions, we consider *grade-level designations, instructional planning, language program placements, working hours, parent communication,* and, interwoven throughout, the *place of children* in the school itself. We begin by highlighting this last aspect of institutional life; that is, we consider, to whom do the children belong?

Throughout our discussion, we refer to literacy—and to writing in particular; these literacy threads will be part of the fabric of our experiences in this second chapter of our document and brought to the foreground for closer examination in the third and fourth chapters.

Reputations, Expectations, and the "Hall" Children

All of us, to varied degrees, thought of our classrooms as "homes," as kinds of "families"—but our feelings about our *schools* were more varied. In Linda's words, "If you just talk about inside the classroom, your teaching, there are wonderful stories. But if you get a little bit farther outside the door. . . ."

Outside the door we experienced schoolwide cohesiveness, or its lack, in the ways children themselves figured into both informal and formal collegial talk. Most revealing were "difficult" children, children who stretched the school's social and academic norms. Children so perceived could be included, or excluded, jointly embraced, or blamed on particular teachers or family stereotypes. Indeed, such children could sometimes be perceived in our school halls—in these temporary holding zones for children—as interfering with the work of the school, rather than *as* the work of the school.

Andrea's Patsy was one such child:

Andrea: This is [Patsy's] second year with me, but she came to me last year because she was in another class and the teacher could not deal with her any longer, so we swapped children. . . . So when she came back the first day of school she walked up to me and she said, "I was really surprised when I saw my name on your list." I asked why and she said, "Because I thought you didn't like me last year, and you let me in your class again so that must mean you like me." And I said, "Yes, Patsy, I like you." . . . No [other teacher] will take her. They tell me all the time, "Do not give her to me. I'm glad I didn't get her."

Anne: That's interesting, too. Children who get reputations.

Judy: Especially bad ones.

Linda: Andrea has a reputation for taking all those kids.

Anne: Ah, the reputation of the *teacher*.

Andrea: But I have a sense of humor with them. . . . I had the whole class, as a matter of fact, assess themselves. It was interesting, the things that she wrote about herself.

An interest in what children had to say about themselves seemed to pervade a school that Linda had visited. The school had inspired her, she said, because "it was completely supportive of the child."

Linda: Whatever adult was nearby . . . sat down with that child and talked to that child about whatever issue it was, and [the children] had to write what they had to do differently. The whole thing was problem solving, not punitive. It was not, "OK, you're getting expelled" or "we're getting your parents in here." . . . But the whole staff totally supported this model, so the resource teachers, the librarian, the custodian, the secretary—

Judi: The principal—

Linda: I mean the whole school was moving together. . . . It was beautiful, so inspiring to see this positive environment.

Carolyn: You know, I'm listening, and all of this relates. At our site . . . I hear celebrations when certain children leave [my] school. It's almost as though that's what we work towards: making life miserable for their folks. And so then their folks finally say, "I've had it. Call me one more time at my job and we're out of here." And people say, "Call them; let's get them out." Then when they go it's like, "Good luck to School X because now they have them." It's not the answer. That's what I find that bothers me.

This bothered all of us, and we often chose for study children who defied their own "reputations." Jill, for example, found second-grader Katherine much more complex, much more interesting than her reputation had suggested:

Jill: [Katherine] started at our school last year in first grade. Her first-grade teacher shared with me, saying "Katherine's very inattentive." She classified her as an Attention Deficit child. "She can't sit still, and she's all over the place. . . . She can't focus on any specific activity for longer than five minutes. She can't read. She can't write." So I got this long list of "she can'ts." I said, "Can you give me some of her strengths?" "Well, she's sweet." "Give me more." "She's very loving, and she likes to draw." So she felt like those

FIGURE 3 | TAKING TIME FOR TALK: JUDY DEEP IN CONVERSATION.

were her only strengths. So Katherine came this year to second grade . . . and it *was* hard for her to pay attention but we found different ways. We'd move her every ten or fifteen minutes. "Sit over here with somebody," and then, "OK, now you're ready to come up and move." But what I came to find out is that she . . . really was anxious to write, and to learn how to write. Well, I felt like she already knew how to write, so it was acknowledging her skills that she already had that really helped her to gain some confidence and self-esteem.

In our experiences, *children* with "reputations" could be blamed on *parents* with reputations, stereotypical ones. Indeed, some of us were reluctant to discuss children's backgrounds with colleagues—and others, like Elise and Judi, felt no such reluctance. Still, Judi remembered feeling differently:

Judi: [Our] whole school was founded on the basis of making education accessible to Latino families in Oakland. . . . I think that their sensitivity to meeting the needs of Spanish-speaking children extends to meeting the needs of all . . . groups. So if someone were to make remarks that were stereotypic or that reflected insensitivity, they know that these would not be accepted by other members of the faculty. . . . I think that, in reading what the kids write, you can see that . . . because of the freeness the kids feel to write about what they write about and also in the way that they write. But I have been in other schools where it wasn't like that. . . . People will say . . . "What do you expect? Mexican families don't value education. No wonder."

Anne: Well, when the Secretary of Education said that not too long ago. . . .

Judi: He's only reflecting what some of his colleagues surely think if they don't say. . . . Sometimes, I think teachers make remarks like that because it sort of excuses them. It is a frustration. . . . Because there are challenges in teaching. When a teacher is working with children who are not from his cultural or linguistic experience, it is still more challenging. . . .

Carolyn: I guess I am the opposite of Judi. I was at a school where we talked about problems with children. Because this school was so small, we knew a lot of the families. . . . I felt comfortable discussing background information and knowing that it was going to be used for instructional purposes and the kids weren't going to be judged on any negative information [e.g., about family breakups, economic strains, substance abuse or the like].

Where I am now . . . I don't feel that comfortable. . . . This year in September, one of the second-grade teachers came up to me in the hall and asked if I had had this particular child. I said, "Yes." Then she said, "What's wrong with her?" That was how she greeted me. I was really taken aback. I said, "Well she was fine when I had her. What exactly do you mean?" Then she went on to speak particularly about the child's skills in writing. This was like the second week in school. . . . I gave her no information. . . . I didn't feel comfortable because of the way that I was approached. The teacher had already assumed that there had to be something wrong with this child.

For us, then, a pervasive feeling of collegiality is linked to a feeling of joint responsibility for the school's children. When each teacher "owns" her own children, when her reputation depends upon their behavior (for her alone, not necessarily for others) and upon their "readiness," as it were, for the next teacher's class, then children perceived as too different can be threats, children whose words, actions, and behaviors grind against the edges of their assigned place in the system. When the children belong to all of us, then new possibilities emerge, possibilities born of child respect and teacher collaboration—stories like many of those we will share in the pages ahead.

Designated Grade Levels, Retention, and the "Tall" Children

"He was almost a hall child," said Judy one day about second-grader Alberto, a child who, she felt, had "really [been] in danger of losing himself."

Judy: Alberto always wants to argue with me about everything, and he's very good at it. . . . He's fun to talk to, but he's one of those kids who makes you want to say, "I love what you're saying, but could you go away for a minute because you're driving me crazy?". . . I had him in kindergarten, but he went to another teacher for first grade last year, and I used to see him sitting out [in the hall] a lot. . . . When he came back to me this year, I could tell that he had lost some of his sense of who he was. . . . His teacher focused on [the sound/symbol skills Alberto did need help with but] didn't really see what Alberto had learned already, how bright he was. . . . Today Alberto [who is Spanish dominant] . . . fixed [the computer] all by himself. And he was so excited, he lay on the floor, shouting, "Voila!" He wouldn't stop, and I looked down at him finally and said, "You better get up, you're starting to speak French!"

Like his first-grade teacher, Judy found Alberto talkative, argumentative, and still grappling with the nature of the alphabetic system, but she also found him interested in ideas, a sound reasoner, and a fine poser and solver of problems. Alberto would not fit comfortably in a slot designed for the "normal" second grader—he's "too smart" as an oral debater, "too slow" as a reader and writer, and he has technological skills that "don't count" in the second grade.

More than any other aspect of institutional life, these grade-level "norms" mediate our sense of ourselves and our students and, moreover, students' sense of their own competence, as Carolyn remarked:

Carolyn: [S]ometimes we really have to take a look at the system. An example is we have kindergarten checklists, and we need to take a look at what's on there to see if those are things we really want children to know before they can go on to first grade. Other things need to be taken into consideration. I've seen children who are as tall as I am in third grade, who really feel like the oddballs.

And so Carolyn paved the way for Allen, one of Carol's case-study children. Allen was a sweet-tempered child—a tall child, who loomed over his peers, and who also had overcome enormous difficulties to be there, everyday, working hard, in Carol's class.

Carol: I guess this all kind of fits in relation to the person that I have. His name is Allen. He's a kid whose mother was on drugs for a while, and this poor little kid had to be on his own. He was not in school for like a year and a half, and he was moving from place to place. He was one of those kids that lost a whole year. So he came to my school last January. It's his second year. He was one of those kids who did not know his ABC's, nothing. He could barely write his name, literally. . . . [To add to the difficulties] the kid's not been able to sleep because of the [new] baby. He sleeps in the same room with the baby . . . and he comes everyday. He tries hard. . . . What he's doing now, which I feel really good about, is . . . this is the first story that *he's* initiated. . . . But I just feel so frustrated that it's a little tiny step.

Louise: Is your biggest worry what's going to happen next year [in fourth grade]?

Carol: Yes.

Louise: That would scare me.

Carol: I worry that someone will see him and think, "Oh he can't do it. . . ."

Carolyn: Is there any way that you can talk to the fourth-grade teacher?

Carol: Yes. . . . In fact, there are at least seven kids in other classes who are going on [and are in a similar situation as Allen].

Carolyn: And this is where I feel the system fails the kids. Why should he have to fit into the system?

Carol: Right.

Carolyn: How do we make [the system] work to fit kids?

Carol: How do you have these kids have a place?

Louise: And how could you keep him next year and have him be in fourth grade? Why couldn't he continue in your class and be in fourth grade?

Evident in our discussion is the way in which grade levels mediate the space allowed both teachers and children for negotiating vertical differences. To renegotiate this space, Carol needed the cooperation, and the collegial support, of teachers at her site. Indeed, her "biggest worry" was that Allen's progress will be disrupted and, potentially, discounted.

For all of us, possibilities for negotiating grade-level boundaries were linked to the interest of colleagues occupying the other side of the borders. At Judy's school, teachers were collaboratively exploring multiage classrooms designed to eliminate, or at least reduce, grade-level labelling—something that does not necessarily happen when, for example, "first" and "second" graders are combined to meet the exigencies of the moment, to "even out the numbers" of children in each teacher's slot. Moreover, many of us were keeping children across two or more years, as Carol had done with Allen. Andrea's comments below typify our feelings.

Andrea: I wish I had [my kids] for third, fourth, and fifth. One year I had a fourth, fifth, and sixth, and it was beautiful. I kept some students for two years. Some didn't blossom 'til the end of the second year, so it was really nice.

And whatever the grade or level designation, we were concerned that "other things be taken into consideration" in defining the competence of individual children. As evidenced by our constructions of case histories, we were interested in the "whole child," in holistic assessments that attempted to catch what too often "fell between the cracks" of report cards and standardized tests. That stuff in the crevices may be just the artistic or social skills, the "funds of cultural knowledge" (Moll, Amanti, Neff, & Gonzalez, 1992), or the critical perspective on the taken-for-granted that allows us new visions of individual children's resources and new ways to engage children in our classrooms.

Open Doors and Opening Minds in Instructional Planning

As we finished our extended discussion of Carol's Allen, and our consideration of the ways grade levels could be negotiated, Linda had a suggestion:

Linda: I just wanted to share what Andrea and I have started doing. She has 3rd/4th combination, and I have kindergarten, and we've started a cross-age tutoring program. . . . And then today I did a "100 day" project with my kids where they had to bring 100 of something to count. So I said "Andrea, I need four kids," and she sent me her students, and they helped my kindergartners count. It was so nice in the classroom, having these older kids there. . . . So it's really nice. . . . The kids that need so much attention have somebody giving them attention. . . . So that was what I was thinking, even as far-fetched as it may sound, if he could become a tutor?

When collegial relationships existed, we as teachers were more able to exploit the resources of, and meet the needs of, the school's children. Instructional planning need not be confined to "grade-level" curricula or, even, individual teachers' lesson plan books. Thus Linda made the not-at-all "far-fetched" suggestion that Allen become a tutor, developing his literacy abilities by sharing them with younger children. Her relationship with Andrea allowed both teachers to take advantage of the value the older children placed on helping the young, a value evident in many of our working-class and minority neighborhoods.

Judi, who literally described her school as a "family," spoke with pride about the school literary magazine, which included the drawing and writing of children from kindergarten through sixth grade. During one of our teas, she read us the "Dear Readers" letter written by two fifth-grade members of the Literary Magazine Board:

Judi: "Dear Reader. Welcome to the literary magazine. This here magazine will make you want to jump up and down with joy. . . . We spent a lot of time to make this book just so you could read [it]. . . . Please don't throw this book into a trash can. . . . We got a lot of different cultures writing. Some of the writing was hard to read and understand because students wrote their own way of writing English. . . . Thanks for your support. . . ."

After listening to these stories of collaborative support among teachers and children, Carolyn remarked that her school was "more of an individual classroom with your own door," both literally and figuratively, which she regretted. In one teaching story in particular, she illustrated the value of opening those doors:

Carolyn: It was the week of St. Patrick's Day and in my lesson plans I decided I was going to talk about . . . leprechauns. [But] when I mentioned leprechauns, my class went berserk. They said, "We know leprechauns. They are mean and ugly." . . . Then they started to talk about this movie that was on HBO. I went home and I looked in the TV guide, and my sister and I talked about it. . . . It was very violent. . . .

I tried to counteract what they were saying. . . . There is . . . a teacher with fourth graders, who had a bulletin board up with leprechaun stories that they had written, and they were quite good, with pictures. So I took [my children] down, and [we] looked at their bulletin board. Then about four of the students from [that] fourth-grade class came down to our classroom, and they read their stories to us. They talked to the children about some of the things that they had learned, like leprechauns were tricksters and if you caught [one], then they had to grant you three wishes. . . .

One of the kindergarten teachers said that she knew a woman who was from Ireland . . . and I relayed [that to my children]. So I said, "There are people who think that they really believe in leprechauns. . . . I told them that this was a part of their culture, and they know how they feel about things that are important to their family and who they are.

Carolyn's story highlighted *informal,* spontaneous collaborations, rather than more formally planned ones, and, like Judi's, it illustrated the value of extending, in addition to tapping, common experiences and values. There is a connection between opening classroom doors and opening children's minds. When all of us, children or adults, interact with people who have different experiences, different values, we have the potential for experiencing "culture," for understanding differences by finding similarities: "You know how you feel about things important to your family," Carolyn told her children. "We got a lot of different cultures," wrote Judi's Board Members, and they all were writing "English." Both informal collaborations and more formally planned ones, both exploiting cultural differences and tapping common values, depend on dialogue among school "family" members, upon knowing what each other is doing.

Of course, we ourselves were a collegial group. And it is not surprising, perhaps, that a collaborative endeavor, involving difference as resource, arose from our group. One day, in the midst of a class discussion of a child's "Bruce Lee" story (based on the film about the karate expert and movie star), Kristin's third grader, Letty, asked why there was no "Africatown," given that there was a "Chinatown." The ensuing discussion (which gave rise to many more) revealed misconceptions about Chinese Americans—including that they were not "Americans." Since there were very few children of Chinese heritage at Kristin's school, she took advantage of Elise's invitation to the group to come visit at her school, to meet her kindergartners:

Kristin: Elise met [my children and me] . . . and walked us through Chinatown to her school, and we did a lesson with her kids. We made a red envelope for [Chinese] New Year, and it was really fun.

Elise: The kids were polite; they all played so well!

Kristin then explains that one of her children, Sammy, who is African American, would not sit down with Elise's children at first.

Kristin: He said, "Those kids aren't going to like me because I'm Black. They only like white kids."

Judi:　　　Oh my gosh.

Kristin:　　I went to Elise, and she picked out with great care a Black boy and his best friend, who is Chinese, and we walked him over, and I said, "Sammy, Elise has someone who she wants you to meet." And we introduced [Sammy to the other Black child]. And I saw Sammy's face! [Kristin beams]. . . . And then I said, "And this is his best friend." And then he went over and sat down with them. And then afterwards, the next day, we wrote about the field trip . . . and Sammy shared that he had first been scared.

This is, of course, a story with a happy ending—but learning about (and living in) a world of differences does not have a "then-they-lived-happy-ever-after" ending. Whether we are teachers trying to figure who needs what, or children trying to figure out who plays with whom, negotiating differences is an ongoing aspect of everyday life. But stories, like Linda's, Judi's, Carolyn's, and Elise and Kristin's, allowed us to articulate those moments when we were positively and collaboratively managing institutional structures (e.g., individual classrooms, grade levels, and even school populations) to make a difference amidst differences.

Language Placements and Ethnic Circles

In many of our schools there is another sort of institutional structure to be negotiated, that of institutionalized language placements or programs. As our child populations have become increasingly linguistically diverse, our efforts to take advantage of, and meet the needs of, our children have been both supported and made complex by state- and districtwide efforts. As financially strapped urban districts work to meet changing guidelines, as certification requirements and, indeed, the names of those requirements come in and out of fashion, collegial tensions may arise. Teachers designated "monolingual" or "bilingual," "Sheltered English" or "Language Development Specialists," "Spanish reading" teachers or "Cantonese literacy" people may feel that their responsibilities for their "own" children pit them against the teachers of the "others."

Moreover, these faculty divisions may exacerbate children's own divisions, an observation also made by the ethnographer Grace Guthrie (1992). Out on some of our playgrounds the children themselves clique together within racial and ethnic circles, a phenomenon that seems to increase as children move through the grades. That young children find comfort with familiar faces, voices, and experiences is *not* a problem. But when those faces, voices, and experiences are not contributing to a larger school world, when children's social and intellectual worlds are not contributing to each other's expanding world view—their cultural "happening" so to speak—and when the school itself seems to contribute to the children's distance from each other and, perhaps, from the school itself, then we do find this a problem, a troubling one. As Elise said, the children become "stifled in their knowledge of other people."

We have no magic answers to these dilemmas, but we do know that bringing teachers together in dialogue is key in building joint responsibility for all children, whatever one's own special contributions, as Judy's experiences illustrate. Judy felt very comfortable at her school, as if she "belonged" there. But still there were tensions between bilingual and monolingual teachers, tensions that contributed to racial tensions among the teachers themselves. While these tensions were not fully resolved, her faculty did develop a plan that incorporated the talents of all their teachers for all their children:

Judy: We didn't have enough bilingual teachers, so some of our staff would have had to leave. So instead of leaving, they split up the groups and intermingled them in the afternoons. So in the morning actually I'm two bilingual teachers because I have a totally bilingual class or a totally primary language instruction class. But in the afternoon, because I did that, the other teacher who is not bilingual will have half of my kids. So it [this combining and recombining of children] was a way to keep all the staff and not to hire new people.

Through collaborative engagement in projects, like managing a classroom store or exploring those computers Alberto was so fond of, children themselves made new connections. Moreover, Judy herself came to "belong" to diverse children—as Elizabeth and Anne noticed when they visited her school. Out on the playground, children from first through sixth grade, of varied colors and language rhythms, came by to drape themselves around Judy, a cross-cultural elementary schoolchild kind of hug.

Working Hours, Door Keys, and Paperwork

Informal interactions, collegial projects, schoolwide planning—all involve not only institutional flexibility but also time and trust, as we reiterated time and again. Our narratives of classroom life often revealed a lack of time for each other, and even for the sort of mundane tasks Carolyn Steedman reminisces about in the opening epigraph—rummaging among materials, finding a special book, recording stories, planning displays, rethinking the placement of desks and of children—an ongoing list of never-ending tasks.

On discouraging days the regulated environment of urban schools can feel overwhelmingly stiff; we are to sign in and sign out, get there on time, and leave on time, and, in the middle, follow the directions. Through these daily actions, we form our sense of how we figure into the social order of schools, of the limits on our professional decision-making power:

Carolyn: If we have three days without students, we are not trusted to organize our time. . . . So if I decide to change my bulletin board, they [the administrative staff] wouldn't consider that to be productive. If I decided to listen to some records to decide which one to use with my kids, then that is not a good use of time. But if you give me some forms and I have to turn them in, then you'll know that I really did attend to something that had to do with education. . . . [And] I get kicked out at four. Our custodian leaves and the building has to be locked up. . . .

Judi: In our school . . . they set the alarm system before they make us leave. There's not even an alarm on my [portable] and I stay there after [hours] all the time. [The custodian is] always kicking me out. . . . [Someone mentions a teacher who has a *key* to her suburban school.] I don't think any of us have [a key]. Because there are some safety issues. . . .

Linda: And we've been begging our principal to at least let us come in on a Saturday so we can work in our rooms when there's no kids around. . . .

Carolyn: A sad story is another teacher and I, one Friday, really wanted to stay after school. We had things we were working on we needed to finish, and we stayed in my room, turned off the lights, and let them lock the building up so that we could then stay and do our work. . . . I can see the hazard also if we got hurt, or someone came in and assaulted us in some way. But I mean, we're two adults; we're not going to let someone in the door who we don't know. . . . And I thought, how ironic, that I'm hovering in the room, in the dark, waiting for someone to leave, so that I can work overtime.

Linda: That you're not getting paid for. . . . Just think, a boss who has a worker that wants to do extra work, that wants to do the job better, and you get punished for being like that. It's crazy.

Elise: That's why I have [parent conferences] at 7:30 before school . . . whenever I can get them in.

In the main, we have little time allotted during the day for individual or joint planning. Moreover, our schools are not, overall, community centers; they are locked up after hours, and we are to lock our individual doors and go home. It can be hard not only to interact with each other but also to interact with our parents, as Elise's comments illustrate. While some of our schools have days reserved for parent conferences, others do not; teachers squeeze parents in as they can at the beginning of the day or the end—times when most parents are working.

"Can you imagine," asked Carolyn, "you start at 7:30, and then you go through your teaching day, and then you end the teaching day and hurry the kids out because you've got someone else coming at 3:15 and you've got to be out of the building by 4:00?"

"No wonder people do dittoes," said Marty.

"I don't have time to run dittoes," replied Judi.

And we all laughed.

But we all took quite seriously the way in which the institution of the school mediated our relationship with our parents, as we discuss below.

Conferences, Chats, and Eating Soup

When Elizabeth and Anne visited Judy's primary classroom, they met Dahlia, a soft-spoken, bright-eyed six-year-old. Judy had asked her children to write about themselves, and they were circulating, chatting with the children about their work. Dahlia had drawn a Nicaraguan flag on the top of her paper and, then, a Mexican one. When Anne knelt down beside her, Dahlia talked animatedly about people and places in Mexico and Latin America—and Anne was completely lost within seconds. Her difficulty wasn't due to Dahlia's Spanish dominance; it was due to differences in their cultural and personal field of reference. It would have taken many conversations, not a quick interaction, to figure out her life spaces and significant others.

Anne's experience with Dahlia emphasizes the importance of interaction between parents and teachers, of knowing something of young children's lives outside the classroom. It is hard to share language when experiences are not shared and, strangers, for whom loved ones' names and familiar places sound odd and distant, are likely to remain strangers. All of our presented case studies illustrated the potential value of knowing about children's lives outside school.

And yet, such interaction seemed increasingly hard to achieve. When we talked about variation in our experiences as teachers, both over time and across schools, the most consistently mentioned change was the nature of the relationship between home and school. As urban schools have become more financially stressed, the wealth of neighborhood parents—and the involvement of those parents in local public schools—have had an impact on our daily teaching experiences.

At one of Carolyn's former schools, for example, "the parent group . . . raised lots of money, and teachers got individual stipends from the parent group to purchase materials. . . . [At my most recent school], we felt like it was principal, teachers, kids, and basically that was it." In Kristin's school, which served socioeconomically and culturally very different neighborhoods, Kristin experienced pressure from the more affluent parents, who tended to closely monitor the curriculum and instruction offered their children (and who, if unhappy, could and did withdraw to private schools); and she felt distanced from the less affluent parents, who tended to live further away from the school and whose lives and resources (e.g., transportation, time, and money) made such involvement more problematic.

FIGURE 5 | WORKING TOGETHER IN ELISE'S ROOM.

Moreover, fewer parents were home during the day. For Elise, this had been the biggest change in her teaching experience—"the mothers going out to work. The Chinese mother not being at home. . . . They have this conflict between being at home and then wanting to take part in the Western culture," a culture itself in conflict, with schools dependent on mothers who do not work outside the home and who are able to contribute time and money, and socioeconomic and cultural circumstances that make those dependencies often unrealistic.

Indeed, our schools sometimes function as poorly staffed social service centers for economically troubled neighborhoods. Written forms go home for one service or another, forms that are often hard to read, invasive, or potentially insulting—a "communication" strategy that seems designed to increase the distance between home and school.

Carolyn: [Parents could be receiving Aid to Families with Dependent Children (AFDC) but not] submit the applications for their children to receive the free/reduced lunch. . . . So a lot of that paperwork that goes home, those forms, they don't fill that stuff out because they feel as though their child is going to be categorized. . . . And then sometimes . . . if it's a custodial parent instead of a biological parent, they don't know how to fill these forms out, or they just don't. So it's sometimes negligence that these kids are hungry and they're not getting food because no one will fill out the forms for them.

Jill: The forms are also intimidating. They're very, you know, small print, four copies, and the carbon copies. . . .

Carolyn: [And then] it doesn't appear to be very confidential. . . . And it has all of their personal business on it: how many kids they have, the ages of those kids, what their income is, and all of that.

Added to increased socioeconomic stresses—and the bureaucratic means of addressing some of those stresses—was the ever increasing linguistic and cultural diversity of our parents. For example, many of Elise's students did not live in the neighborhood but were cared for by varied extended family members who did reside there. Elise found it challenging to remember the different family members who might come for a child. Further, in a number of cases, the children's families spoke neither Cantonese nor English, Elise's own languages, and she needed the assistance of children's older siblings, or instructional aides, to talk with them.

To add to the complexity (and the cultural richness), the children's families sometimes had assumptions about the teacher's role that differed from mainstream expectations; they expected Elise to help them discipline the child at home (rather than the more typical teacher request for parental help with school discipline).

Elise: Phi Long [who is Vietnamese] is taken care of by a lot of adults. The grandmother brings him, the mother comes in, the father comes in, his older sisters pop in. . . . And the mother wanted me to tell him not to play with video games every night. She said, "He really listens to you. You tell him to only play with video games

> on Friday." And then, "Tell him to eat his soup." . . . So I told him for her. I said, "You bring me the soup if you don't want it, because I like soup." And then I asked her if he eats soup now, and she said, "Oh, yes. Oh, yes." And we talked about the video games on Fridays.

Despite the apparent need for opportunities to come to know and appreciate children's out-of-school lives, as a group we found little institutional support for such opportunities. As we discussed above, parent-teacher conferences were not institutionally provided for in all of our schools, unless teachers themselves used personal leave days for such conferences, or squeezed them in at the beginning or end of the day. Indeed, one of Carolyn's parents reported that, when she mentioned to "her cousin who had a child at the school for six years that she was coming to a parent conference, she said, 'When did they start doing that?' I nearly died."

Given this lack of support, informal contacts seemed especially important. Such contacts were most available to kindergarten teachers, whose parents more often accompanied their children to and from school. It was this sort of regular, informal contact (combined with her years of service at the same school) that helped Judi come to know the complex home situation of kindergartner Anita, whose stories were as complex as Judy's Dahlia.

Judi: In kindergarten the parents drop the kids off, they're right there, and so I got to know [Anita's father] because I had [one brother] for two years, and I had the other son. So I got to know him. We'd talk in the mornings when he'd bring them. When his wife died I tried to express sympathy as best as I could. It was so hard for him. Anita was a baby, and he had to go back and forth to the hospital and try to get the boys to school on time. . . .

[On the tape I brought today, Anita is telling stories about her family.] If you notice, she'll get confused if she's talking about her dead mom or the mom who lives now. Because the mother who lives now is from El Salvador, but her other mom is from Mexico. She talks about how she has a sister in El Salvador, but this is really the daughter of her mother now. . . .

While we did not all enjoy such close and easy relationships with parents, all enjoyed and, moreover, found important affirmation in such relationships, as the narratives below suggest:

Linda: [For me as a kindergarten teacher, the parents are] right there. When I see them, everyday, those little one-minute comments [are great].

Carolyn: I totally agree. Just the fact that some of the parents that you're talking about, like the drop-in today. I had the chance to have a thirty-minute conversation, and how rich and how validating. . . . I needed to know how the interview went when [the children] had to go find out what [their] parent did as a child for Halloween. I needed to know that that was something the parent enjoyed doing with their child. . . . I let her ask the questions, I interacted with her, I gave her as much information as I could, I let her give me information about her child, and it was wonderful. . . .

Louise: And don't you think you'll feel differently about the child?

Carolyn: Absolutely.

Louise: You have such a different feeling about a child who you know in those ways.

For most of us, such feelings came from our own reaching out, a particularly necessary action when teachers hope to form bonds with children whose families differ from their own in socioeconomic circumstance, race or ethnicity, language, and culture. As Andrea and Louise pointed out,

Andrea: Sometimes I'll hear teachers say, and I'm thinking of other cultures [of teachers who work with children of cultures other than their own]—I'll say, "Well did you call home?" And they'll say, "No." "A whole year and you haven't called the home? Did you send a letter?" "No." "You have to. . . ."

Louise: If you can't be friendly with the kids' parents, it's awfully hard for the kids then. Why should the kid trust you if you can't be nice to the parents?

Working toward such trust—interacting with families from diverse socioeconomic, cultural, and linguistic backgrounds—could be the source of rich information about children and, indeed, a source of our own continual cultural happening, our own learning, and it could also be the source of frustration. The degree to which it was one or the other depended, in part, on the ways in which schools provided institutional support for our efforts, or the ways in which we were able, nonetheless, to circumvent institutional rigidity.

Summary: "Who Am I to Them?"

In each of our classrooms, our relationships to our own students are mediated by our relationships with adults outside our classroom doors. Within the institutional structure of schools, each teacher, each child, each child's family has their designated slot, their place in the system. The flexibility or rigidity of that system is realized in, or countered by, our own actions, our own efforts to negotiate these slots and thereby better meet the needs of, and exploit the resources of, our children.

In our experiences, *joint instructional planning,* both formal and informal, and the *grouping of children* across traditional *grade levels* or *language placements* were ways in which instructional and interactional spaces were opened up: vertical differences in children's learning could be more easily allowed for, horizontal differences in personal, cultural, and linguistic knowledge and experience could be more easily transformed into school resources.

Conversely, the tight regulation of our *weekly work hours*—the lack of time for professional reflection and decision making—made us feel like cogs in the system, overwhelmed and, sometimes, alone. Those tight hours could make it difficult to reach out, not only beyond classroom doors, but beyond school walls, to children's families. Current institutional structures can make it too easy to remain strangers to children's social and cultural frames of reference, to their caregivers and siblings, to significant family events.

"Who am I to them?", Andrea asked in telling her story about unruly children and teachers who abruptly entered and left their lives. In a similar way, we have collectively asked, Who are we to the children in our schools? In sharing responsibility, in not being strangers to each other, to students, or to caregivers, we help construct flexible institutions that belong to us all.

Issues We Reflect On

1. **What is "a school community"?**

   a. What evidence exists at your school site that teachers and students feel as if they are members of a "community"?

   b. What evidence exists that families are a part of a school "community"?

2. **What does a collegial school look like? What does it feel like?**

   a. What qualities of a school culture make it "safe" for teachers to openly communicate?

   b. What kinds of formal and informal practices or ways of doing things contribute positively to open relations? What practices work against open relations?

   c. What sorts of issues related to sociocultural difference, language, and literacy should be discussed by school faculty and staff?

   d. How is time for talk structured? How do people learn to talk collegially?

   e. Is it necessary, reasonable, or desirable for teachers to have a stake in all of the children at a school, regardless of separate programs and placements? If so, what school practices further such a sense of responsibility?

3. **How do educators negotiate hierarchical institutional structures for children who fall between the cracks?**

   a. In what ways do educators work within or stretch the boundaries of set instructional programs, assessment tools, and student placement decisions to meet the language and literacy needs of particular children?

   b. What kinds of collaborations among educators contribute to these practices?

4. **What is the nature of the ideal home/school relationship?**

   a. What obstacles do educators and parents face in negotiating an "ideal" relationship?

   b. How do educators become informed about their children's communities, including their resources and culture(s)? What opportunities are available for such learning?

   c. What should be the nature of communication between parents and teachers and, more broadly, community members? What school practices support this communication? Are there any specific practices that help create bridges across socioeconomic, cultural, and linguistic differences between school and community?

5. **What kinds of practices contribute to children's sense of ownership of and pride in their school?**

   a. In your school site, do children participate in activities with those outside their own classrooms? Is such participation educationally important? Why?

   b. Are there any specific school practices that help create bridges across socioeconomic, linguistic, or cultural differences?

Resource Sampler

Cochran-Smith, M. & Lytle, S. (1993). *Inside/outside: Teacher research and knowledge*. New York: Teachers College Press.

> The authors and their collaborators illustrate the value of teacher—"insider"—inquiry for school reform and curriculum development.

Darling-Hammond, L. (1993). Reframing the school reform agenda: Developing capacity for school transformation. *Phi Delta Kappan, 74,* 752–761.

> The definition of "school community" presented in this article is undergirded by the assumptions that students are diverse, that teaching is interactive, and that bureaucratic rules have too often impeded teachers' efforts to "prevent students from falling through the cracks."

Heath, S. B. (1983). *Ways with words: Language, life, and work in communities and classrooms*. Cambridge: Cambridge University Press.

> A unique exploration of the sociocultural differences that can exist among communities only a few miles apart and the ways in which those differences can be played out in schools.

Kozol, J. (1992). *Savage inequalities*. New York: HarperCollins.

> A distressing, eye-opening book about the distribution of resources in "public" education.

Lightfoot, S. L. (1978). *Worlds apart: Relationships between families and schools*. New York: Basic Books.

> An older but still very relevant book on the nature of respectful relations between homes and schools.

Meier, D. (1995). *The power of their ideas: Lessons for America from a small school in Harlem*. Boston: Beacon Press.

> The "powerful ideas" referred to in the title are those of both children and teachers—when they have spaces for dialogue with colleagues, as well as each other.

Chapter **3** | Building Classroom Communities

"I'm from Texas; What Are You?"

It was when I found out I had to talk that school became a misery, that the silence became a misery. I did not speak and felt bad each time that I did not speak. I read aloud in first grade, though, and heard the barest whisper with little squeaks come out of my throat. "Louder," said the teacher, who scared the voice away again. The other Chinese girls did not talk either, so I knew the silence had to do with being a Chinese girl.

M. Hong Kingston, *The Woman Warrior*

In the rhythm of her everyday interactions with teachers and children, author Maxine Hong Kingston simultaneously learned about reading at school and about her identity as a "Chinese girl" in that place. The interactional requirement to read loudly made visible her gender and her ethnicity in uncomfortable ways, just as it made visible her low status as a reader.

The children in our own classroom stories prompted questions, not only about how children were learning to write and to read, but also about what they were learning about themselves in the process. As teachers, we all aimed for a feeling of community in our classrooms, a feeling of being interconnected, engaged in a common enterprise, energized by common goals. And we saw literacy activities as playing key roles in forming such inclusive communities. However, the group dynamics in our classrooms were influenced by the divisions and inequities of the larger society, including the interrelated divisions of race, gender, and class.

Our children, and sometimes we ourselves, felt one aspect of our identity foregrounded in more or less comfortable ways. And degree of comfort was often connected with who was doing the foregrounding, the defining, as Kristin suggested in a story about her class' experience with pen pals:

Kristin: My class [which is predominantly African American and European American] has pen pals down in Southern California, which is suburban LA. . . . We got letters from our pen pals today, and one of them, this little boy, wrote a letter to my student and wrote, "I didn't know [until I saw your photograph that] you were brown. It's OK." . . . [Another] wrote to James, who is Korean, he wrote, "What are you? Are you Chinese? I'm Mexican." . . . But, whenever you ask James, he says, "I'm from Texas."

James in particular resisted others' efforts to define him, even as he seemed to Kristin and to his father (who was African American) to be unsure about his own identity in a race-conscious world, a world where one child could be moved seemingly to assure another about his color.

In this chapter, we consider our efforts to build communities in our classroom, focusing on "what difference difference made" in those efforts, that is, the ways in which we experienced sociocultural richness, or sociocultural tension, in relationships between and among ourselves and our children. We illustrate the importance of *curricular participation,* the way in which classroom activities and literate artifacts became symbols of children's inclusion in, and contribution to, the classroom community. We consider also how our *choices of text content* and *text stance* (i.e., the ways in which that content is discussed) could reverberate in our classes, allowing space for children to define themselves as sociocultural beings, as members of groups important to them. Finally, we focus on the way in which *writing activities figured into interpersonal relations,* offering new ways of playing, teasing, and problem solving.

We frame these themes, however, with a consideration of the "pen pal's" question, turned in on ourselves. That is, we ask: What do the children think we are? And how do we transform "what" to "who"?

On Fairness, Goodness, and "Not [Being] My Mother"

"I was absent one day," Andrea said, as she began a story about a substitute who "was so strict I couldn't believe it," and neither could her children:

Andrea: She walked around the room saying, "Do your work! Do this! Don't move! You can't get up!" In order to do their work, they need to get the material to work. She would not let them move. So they sat there, and I found this letter in my mailbox. I have a little mailbox where the kids write to me. . . . It just told her "If you want a child you should go and have a child. . . . Why don't you be cool?" . . . They were saying, "If you want some children to boss, why don't you have your own kids." It's OK to boss your own kids. They said, "We have a mother." I thought that was so cute.

FIGURE 6 | Andrea and her children at work.

Andrea's children, as third and fourth graders, quite clearly differentiated between teachers and mothers; indeed, they used a classic childhood line for adults overstepping their perceived authority: "You're not my mother." And yet, those of us who taught the youngest of children were sometimes called, in fact, "mommy" or "grandma," as we were taken into the children's familiar circle of trusted adults. And, as our discussion below reveals, that taking in was complicated by the salience of racial and ethnic difference in children's worlds:

Linda: I brought my son to school one day, because he's also in kindergarten, and I stood him up in front of the room to introduce him [to my kindergarten students], and all the kids in my class [who are African American] looked at him, and went "He's white!" They were really shocked that he was white. I said, "And what color am I?" And I think they really had to think about it, that I was white too. It was really shocking. . . . It doesn't fit [that they're attached to a white person] because they do live in a very segregated environment.

Verna: It's also true on the other end as well. I was teaching [kindergarten] many years ago, 1970, and it was 99 percent Caucasian at that time. I brought pictures of my children to school, beautiful big 8 X 10 pictures. We always had sharing, and I said, "This morning I'd like to share something with you." So I held up these photos, and said "These are my children." "But they're Black!" The same thing. . . .

As Andrea's story suggested, in the third grade we were no longer mothers. The children seemed much warier about us as teachers and about each other as well, as Louise noted in her response to Verna:

Louise: And yet you run into that, I most ran into it in third grade, that third grade angst, which is "You only like the white kids," or "You only like the Black kids."

Andrea: Or you only talk to the Spanish children. . . .

Carol: I see that a lot in the third grade. It really comes up a lot. I have kids who are student helpers who get to call on kids for recess and I have kids who will say, "Hey, you are just calling on all the white kids or the Black kids." Then it got to the point where they were saying, "You are just calling all of the second graders or third graders." I had a combination class and we had to alternate, "OK, call a boy, then a girl." They are really concerned about issues of fairness.

Remarks like "Hey, you are just calling on" the "other" kids suggested children's views, not only of us as teachers, but also their perceptions of each other. Children's feelings about fairness often revealed their identification of significant groups in the class and their sense of being in competition with them for our attention and affection. Moreover, the "other" could become someone who had something "wrong," with them, someone who, in reference to teachers' expectations, was not being "good," as we discussed:

Andrea: [I brought *Developing Discipline and Positive Self-Images in Black Children* by] Jawanza Kunjufu. . . . It says a lot, because even being a Black person myself, some of the things that he talks about are things that I have experienced in my own upbringing, but as an educator you tend to move away from that some. Therefore at times you have to bring yourself back into that lifestyle with the children to understand your children. . . . Like, sometimes we get upset with the noise level, and playing the dozens [mutual insulting, especially of one's mother] that they play all the time. We get upset sometimes but they're not fighting, it's just a cultural thing. . . .

I have some children that are quite loud, and they're not fighting or mad or anything. They just talk loud. My son was like that in kindergarten. . . . He still talks loud, believe me. And his teachers still can't get used to him. But this is a 99 percent white environment he's in. So they still can't get used to my son's loudness. But . . . when you're sitting there with someone from another culture, it's like the kids [who are not African American] sometimes sit like this [gaping], just looking at them, like "What is *wrong*?" . . . And it may be like we're saying, just cultural awareness, to understand. . . .

Kristin: [Some of my African American kids], I know that they're with me if they [are verbally responding to me] and if they're not, they're doing what's traditional—they're supposed to stay quiet and listen to the story—then they're probably out there [in space] somewhere. . . . And our librarian is constantly [scolding] if they're responding. And their *thing* is to say something. And I finally had to say to her, "You know, I think they are with you when they're doing that."

For both children and teachers, cultural variation in ways of being and communicating could accentuate categorizations of others. Just as some Black children's verbal responsiveness and playfulness could be judged "bad," so too other children's ways of being could be viewed as indicators of social, moral, or intellectual qualities. As we previously noted, children's very names could be judged as signs of being "un-American," as could their knowledge of languages other than English. Through such judgments, children, like the young Maxine, learn about who they are as cultural beings and as school participants—if they are "smart" or not, "good" or not, treated "fair" or not, as we said as our discussion continued:

Andrea: I'm doing a program review for a school in San Francisco, a Filipino school, and the teachers have told me that [the children are] taught not to be aggressive . . . with adults. . . . Some of [the kids] have a hard time because . . . teachers are pushing them to be more aggressive: "Speak out." "Raise your hand for answers." So what [teachers] are doing now is kind of teaching it a little bit so that they're prepared for that once they get out. But it's really a cultural thing, [the teachers] were telling me. A lot of people didn't know that, that they're taught that.

Judy: I think it's a school culture thing also, that we think that to show that you're intelligent you always have to talk. . . . So we don't give credit to the less visible ones. . . .

Andrea: It sounds like we all need multicultural courses.

Jill: Absolutely.

On the other hand, the assumption of cultural differences that were not salient for the individual child could be troublesome too, as could others' need to make too neat our complicated selves:

Carolyn: Today [in my first grade] . . . Shannon was saying, to Eric, "You're not Black." Eric was just sitting there. Somebody else was saying, "He is [so] Black." It was almost like Eric didn't really know whether he was or not. . . . Then this other kid said, "Well I know I'm Black." Then they got in this conversation for a few minutes, and I just stopped and listened. Then when I sat down, they pulled me in and Shannon said, "Hey Mrs. McBride, is Eric Black?" I said, "Well, he's part African American, yes." Then she said, "Oh." Then Megan said, "Well, I'm white." Megan has blond hair, blue eyes. Then Shannon said, "You're not; you are just fair skinned."

Wanda: For my thesis, I've done a [project in Kristin's room] on the way kids interpret multicultural literature. . . . So, a lot of what you all have said are a lot of the things that I've found. [The children] are struggling with culture. I had James [in my project group], who says he is from Texas. When I was reading [multicultural] books to the kids, they were trying to tell him, "No, you're not. You're Korean."

[One of my project books was] *A Birthday Basket for Tia.* It is about a Mexican American family and [Kristin's student] Edward [who is of Mexican heritage] didn't relate to it at all. . . . The book is about the main character's great-aunt's ninetieth birthday. And they have pinatas, and it was a big celebration, and they were dancing and everything. So I said to him, "Is this how you celebrate birthday parties?" He said "No, we just go out and get a cake and come home and that's it."

Carol: The issue about [James] . . . I know with double heritage—I'm Native American and African American, and there are times when you are younger, and you're pitting one against the other, and you are just, "I'm just me." Maybe this is his answer, to just say, "I'm American," rather than are you this or are you that.

Kristin: His father just came back, he was in the Navy, and he's been more a part of his life lately. His father is concerned because he will take him to his friends' house in East Oakland, and James won't play with the kids around there. . . . His dad was really concerned that he wasn't identifying with the African American culture. He doesn't [play with African American children] at school.

FIGURE 7 | Carolyn consulting with her children.

Issues of our complex identities as members of family and peer groups, as national citizens and human beings, were not just matters we adults grappled with; our children grappled too, not in the effort to untangle the tensions and inequities of the larger world, but in the effort to figure out in the local one who they were, and were not. Thus, in all the ways we detail below, we tried to construct inclusive school communities, communities in which children could draw on their own life experiences, learn about the multicultural nature of American society, and be given ample space to learn about themselves, each other, and us, not as "whats" but as complex "whos."

Frog and Toad, Goosebump Books, and Other Markers of Inclusion

Membership in any group involves some kind of marker, some badge of inclusion, and, in our classrooms, such markers included literate artifacts themselves—books that had been read, products that had been completed, activity materials widely used. Our classroom stories revealed the value both we and our children attached to such markers, and moreover, their importance in building a community.

For example, Katherine, Jill's focal child, had been one of nine children "reconfigured" out of her classroom in the early fall, when her school adjusted class sizes—and then "reconfigured" back in six weeks later. That time of absence translated into curricular activities missed, both literally and emotionally, as Jill explained:

Jill: We'll talk about things, and I'll say, "Remember when we talked about this?" "Oh, we weren't here." Or, "You must have talked about that when we weren't here. . . ." So when [Katherine] came [back] . . . most of the other children had already written [*Frog and Toad* stories]. And [the returning children] felt kind of left out, and they said, "We want to do that too. We want to do the puppet shows [with Frog and Toad], we want to do everything that you've already done." And I said, "Well, it's been six weeks, but that's alright." So [Katherine] paired up with another little girl that also had been reconfigured and they wrote, published, and performed a *Frog and Toad* story too.

The valued artifact, the badge of inclusion, was not always instigated by the teacher. In Linda's kindergarten room an important set of artifacts belonged to "Sizzler," a restaurant play ritual initiated by Kesha, another focal child. During free-choice time, anyone anywhere in the room, in the midst of any particular activity, could be approached by a small child with a pad of paper, ready to provide a child-constructed menu, take an order for a burger and fries, and, eventually, to provide delectable plastic food—and all the children, even the "new" ones (just transferred in), played along.

Both *Frog and Toad* stories and "Sizzler" play were important, not only as markers of the individual child's status as a group insider, but also as an avenue into ongoing interaction. These pretend worlds could be collectively remembered as past experiences, jointly built upon in present endeavors, and even offered as symbols of common ground. As Louise noted, familiar books could serve similar purposes. She commented on her children's ways of "welcoming" already known books when she pulled one out to share. And Carolyn told about her children finding teacher-shared books in the school library, no small feat, given the absence of a school librarian and the presence of books "in stacks and on the floor and everywhere."

Our classroom stories revealed not only children's sensitivity to important class artifacts but also to our own ways of talking, to whether or not we ourselves marked children's contributions, indeed, their very existence. The importance of this verbal marking became poignant for Judi when she taught summer school in a new school. In her regular school Judi's knowledge of families and neighborhoods, of the Spanish language and of Mexican American culture, helped her build connections in her multilingual kindergarten. Indeed, knowing, and helping others learn, different languages was itself a badge of inclusion in that room:

Judi:　　One day this little girl was speaking to Rajesh [who's Indian American and one of Judi's focal children], and she said some words in Spanish and he said to her, "I don't speak your language. I speak another language and English too." . . . The kids really have this concept that they can speak a language and English too, because I have so many bilingual kids. Then . . . another little girl came up and said, "Oh, but he speaks a little Spanish too. He's learned it here with us."

In her monolingual "summer" school, which served primarily African American children, Judi was without the very language diversity that had centered so much of her teaching efforts. Moreover, she was struck by the children's references to neighborhood troubles, their concerns about parked police cars, a pervasive community presence, and their comments on her own whiteness: "I was the minority in that class-room, . . . and [the kids] talked very freely about, well, "You're white, Mrs. Garcia." Building up trust, building a web of connections, took not only time and an engaging school routine, but also an inclusive way of talking, a verbal reaching out:

Judi has just talked about her experiences this summer, how, despite many years of teaching, she still had to work hard to connect to her children:

Jill: But also that you had established a community in your [regular] classroom and that it happened over a length of time. . . . Here [in summer school] these kids knowing they're coming for a very short time. . . .

Judi: And it was really frustrating. . . . Every morning as soon as the bell rang I opened the door and I let the kids in, and I'd try to say hello to each of them. . . . And one morning when I was doing that, there was one little boy, and I didn't say his name, and he said, "You didn't tell me 'Good morning,' Mrs. Garcia." And I said "Oh, I'm so sorry," and then I told him good morning. . . . But, you know, they pick up on things like that.

When Anne, Wanda, and Elizabeth visited teachers' classrooms, they noticed teachers' ways of talking, of verbally marking individual contribution to group effort. In one such visit, Louise led a classroom lesson in which individual child lists of "10 things made of paper in my home" were transformed into a group list. When time grew short, Louise went from receiving each list with great enthusiasm, to making sure she had included one new item from each child. "Great data," she said after each contribution, and the children grinned at each other, quite pleased with themselves. Faye, Louise's focal child, put her arm around the child next to her, who had just shared, and revoiced Louise's praise.

In another such visit, Jill worked hard to teach the children to acknowledge each other's contribution, potential or actual:

Jill is meeting with Shane (who is African American), Katherine (Tongan), Ebony (African American), and Angel (Latino, and a recently "mainstreamed, learning-delayed" child). The group is creating their own animal:

Jill:	What color fur does [your animal] have?
Ebony:	Brownish black.
Shane:	Brown on top.
Ebony:	And brownish on (gesturing), like this.
Jill:	Did anybody ask Angel what he wanted?
Angel:	Like this, in patches (pointing to a reference book).
Katherine:	You want patches (acknowledging Angel's view).
Shane:	I think it should have on the top, I think it should have sharp fur.
Jill:	OK, tell them.
Shane:	I think, on the top, it should have sharp fur.
Ebony:	I don't. What would it use it for?
Jill:	Did you hear what she asked you?
Shane:	Yeah, what to use it for. I think it could use it if for, like if [an enemy] tries to grab it or touch it—MM! Like a porcupine's.
Katherine:	Yeah, but see if someone has to pet it.
Shane:	No. Pet it? This is wild. Nobody's going to take it. Soft fur, it's gone. People, the hunters will take it. . . . I think it should have sharp fur, like to break off stuff.
Ebony:	It could use the teeth for that, and its claws.

FIGURE 8 | ELISE'S CHILDREN PLAYING RESTAURANT.

And on the discussion continues, with Jill monitoring social and academic inclusion, as well as scientific logic, and the children learning to do the same.

We did not necessarily find such inclusion easy to do ourselves. Horizontal differences of language and interactional style, as well as vertical ones of evident skill in particular activities, could complicate our efforts to ensure all children access to markers of academic and social membership. Elise, for example, felt distanced from her Vietnamese children at the beginning of the year. "I feel I can't communicate with these children," she said in one of our early meetings. She had, however, identified Vietnamese-speaking parents who could help her, and she paid great attention to the children's drawings and to their play choices, using any expressive evidence of a child's inner life. Because of those factors we have already mentioned—time, markers of shared experiences, and an inclusive style of interacting during group discussions, she too felt bonds build, a community form.

For all of us, quiet children in particular seemed to disappear, and we needed to monitor our own attention to those disappearing children:

Linda: Lisa [one of her focal children] is persistent and the effort is there. Anyway, this is the kind of kid I worry about a lot. . . . [S]ometimes teachers can't pay attention to somebody like this. You pay attention to the bad actors, and Lisa is quiet. . . .

Carol: Allen's a kid, when I assign—say write in your journal or do this assignment, after I've answered about eight or nine questions I think, "I need to go check with Allen. I need to write with Allen. I need to see what he's doing." . . .

Children like Allen, who, relative to their peers, had less control of literacy activities, presented particular challenges. All of us worked to be flexible in our judgments of what children could and could not do, and to provide varied means of support for their participation:

Andrea: With David, who I have, he could barely read.

Linda: The one that was reading [with my kindergartner] the other day?

Andrea: He had a hard time reading, but he wanted to tutor [one of Linda's kindergartners].

Carol: One thing about this I wanted to say too, we had this Reading Is Fundamental program where the kids could choose a book. Everybody loves these Goosebump [mystery] books, so [the people in charge] were saying, "Only pick out a Goosebump book if you're a good reader, because there's not enough to go around." But my whole class picked out a Goosebump book, and he did

too. . . . [Allen] was just really proud to have a chapter book. . . .
He struggles through anyway and tries to read some of it. . . .

Carolyn: I don't worry so much if a child gets a book they can't read themselves during Reading Is Fundamental, and I usually try to do
some activities in the classroom around the books, and then I will
read the books if kids bring them back. So that's unfortunate that
the librarian said that.

Andrea held practice sessions for her third and fourth graders
before they read to Linda's kindergartners; Carol did not hold Allen to
the unfortunate "good reader" rule; and Carolyn planned class activities
around chosen books, activities in which she herself or child partners
read books—rules were bent, avenues for support opened up, activities
themselves made flexible, all so that the importance of each child, and of
the community itself, would not be compromised.

One potential result of such inclusion, we felt, was the children's
own sense that, in Jill's words, "their voice mattered," they were important members of the classroom community—even when they had those
inevitable bad days. During a "hall walk" with Shane, when he was having peer conflicts of one kind or another, Jill asked him, "'What kind of
person do you think you are?' And he looked at me [this child who
argued so effectively for the "sharp fur"], and he said, 'Well, I'm a good
learner.' And I said, 'Yes, you are, that's right.'. . . He knows how to work
there, and he has a real part."

All of us at one time or another mentioned children's awareness of their "real part" in classroom life and learning. To mention just a
few, Carol reported that her class gave her advice about how work groups
for varied activities should be formed. Linda commented on Kesha's own
report, as she looked over a folder of her class work, that she had learned
how to draw fine girls, who not only had all their appendages, but roller
skates and shorts. Louise characterized Faye as the class "summarizer,"
the one who provided metacommentary on group activities and, also,
her own learning:

Louise: The day that I read a Chinese New Year book, I didn't have a very
pretty cover on it, and after I read it, Faye raised her hand, and

she said, "You know, Louise, when you started to read that book, I didn't think this was going to be very interesting. But now that you've read that book, I'm very interested in Chinese New Year, and I'd like to know more about it."

And Carolyn dutifully reported her focal child Darian's request that she make sure our group understood that learning to write had not been such an easy thing for him:

Carolyn: [Darian] said, "Well you should tell them that at first I didn't get it, and then one day I went home, and then I got it. So that's why I can write this now." And I said, "I'll make sure that I tell them that's what happened."

In our classroom stories, children's awareness of their own learning and its importance was linked to more than individual inclusion in common activities; such child awareness was linked as well to the inclusion of children's sociocultural worlds in common texts, as we describe in the section below.

Southern Trips, Halloween Traditions, and Curricular Relevance

"The kids just went bonkers," said Jill one night, reporting her children's response to the book *Nettie's Trip South* (Turner, 1987). The book is about a young white girl's trip to the South in the 1860s, just before the Civil War. Nettie meets a slave at her hotel: "Tabitha, just Tabitha. I don't have a last name." It was at this point in the book that Jill's children went bonkers:

Jill: "What do you mean she doesn't have a last name? You mean they [slaves] didn't have a last name?" It talks in the book about how a dog or a cat just has a first name. So we got into the whole discussion of how the slaves were made to change their names, and they took the last names of the masters. Well, these children today, they wanted to write letters, they wanted to find out their real names, their African names. We had a big discussion. It was incredible. . . . The interesting thing that came up was, "Why hasn't someone told us this before? Why hasn't my mother told me this before? Why hasn't my dad? Why hasn't my aunt and uncle? No one's ever talked about this before." . . . They were shocked. We have two African children in the room, and then they realized, they said, "Oh, so they have their . . . real African names." But it was just all the "Ah ha!'s."

It was that sense of discovery, of "lights going on," that Jill stressed as she described her children. She felt that her children's access to a new perspective on both the past and the present jarred their awareness of their own education, their own need for knowledge. She had, in fact, emphasized a similar reaction when she told us about her children's response to a story in which "a woman gives her husband her jewels to pay for something":

Jill: They asked why she didn't just pay herself, instead of having her husband pay for her. So we talked all about it: why she might have had to do that, whether she'd have to if the story took place now.

Louise: [Those critical questions] are also important because [they] give ideas a level of importance. So many times, ideas aren't valued in the classroom.

Indeed, in many of our group stories, we linked the provision of diverse perspectives in diverse texts, both fiction and nonfiction, with children's awareness of themselves and their world. Such a link, such a grappling with ideas, did not come about automatically but through the "big discussions" they inspired. For example, Carol prompted such discussions through her social studies and literature curricula:

FIGURE 9 | Carol and her children talking science.

Carol: Right now we're doing a unit on Black cowboys of the West. . . . I focus a lot on forgotten heroes. We bring stories of women, Native Americans, others who have been left out of the traditional histories. So we don't separate different parts of history, but everyone's included in the same picture. We talk about the roles of people who haven't been recognized for what they did, and how we can write history to include everyone. Also how our picture of history changes over time. [I try to teach] kids to think critically about what they read and to look for who's included and what's left out.

In some ways, the provision of such curricular breadth was a classroom response to wider educational dialogues about cultural relevance, as we discussed the evening Urvashi Sahni visited. An educator and graduate student from India, Urvashi had discussed her own efforts to make primary curricula responsive to rural Indian children and, like us, she placed great emphasis on children's perspectives:

Urvashi: In all of this culturally appropriate stuff really, what makes me mad is that there's nowhere that they mention kids. It's always adults. . . . I was speaking to a [foreign student] and he was talking about this whole feminist thing. He said, "It's against our culture. . . ." I said, "What do you mean?. . . Let's talk to [the] women and find out how much it's against their culture. . . . I don't know about the females, and I don't know about the kids." . . . I think it's more a case of power really than culture. . . . As long as you don't include people in the participation of planning [including kids] . . . it's just not going to work. . . .

Carolyn: I think one of the reasons that cultural relevance has come up, or Afrocentric curriculum and things of that nature, is because people are now beginning to say, "Well, why are we reaching for that dominant culture's theories?. . . We've not been getting . . . respect." So I think that's the issue there. . . . It's because they don't feel like they've been included in the decision making. . . . I know in my own school, there's a lack of respect for differences of any kind. And when that happens, how can children learn in environments like that, when they're not [respected], not just their cultural background but if they're disabled, if there's economic differences?

Thus, one aspect of cultural relevance and respect had to do with making *children's* present worlds the substance of group-generated texts. This was one dimension of Louise's class compilation of child lists

of "things made of paper" and, also, of Carolyn's "Halloween" activity
discussed below:

Carolyn: Kids nowadays, because of TV shows, and those talk shows, they
know a lot about what an interview is. So we [my first graders
and I] talked a lot about what interviewing is. . . . So they took
home a little sheet that just had some questions, and they would
either ask a grandparent or any adult—someone over 18—
because sometimes people just aren't available to them. . . . The
questions were like, what kinds of treats did you have for Halloween? What costumes do you remember wearing? Did you go to
any Halloween parties, and what were they like? What were some
of the games that you played? And then the kids brought this in,
and we talked about things like bobbing for apples, which was
foreign to a lot of the kids. We talked about some of the costumes
like Felix the Cat, things from a long time ago. And kids then had
these wonderful discussions with their parents. And kids came in
and said, "My mom did this and this."

Louise: That's wonderful. I can't wait till next Halloween!

Carolyn: What happens is it bridges that gap between the parent's childhood and what their child is going through now, and it really
fosters that language about, you know, "When I was a kid I did
this." And we made a chart of the candy that they hoped to get
for Halloween. . . . But then the candy and treats that the parents
got were like popcorn balls and Pez candies. . . . It took a couple of
days to go through and let each kid stand up and tell the class
what they found out, using this little [sheet] as their notes. . . . But
there were problems in that when you can't stay after school to
type the form up, to get it duplicated, and those kinds of things.
And those are the kinds of problems I run into.

The institutional problems of working hours and tightly sched-
uled days we have earlier discussed. But other "problems," issues in
children's everyday lives, surfaced both directly and indirectly when we
worked to include children's sociocultural worlds in our common curricula. Indirectly, activities that involved children's elders had to be sensi-
tively structured, for, like homework itself, they could do harm rather

class and one that led to complex discussions about gender roles and about the nature of power.

All of these literacy avenues—those directed to teachers and those directed to peers, those highlighting children's real worlds and those displaying their imagined ones—revealed and contributed to our complex relationships with children, and their relationships with each other. Andrea captured the complexity of these relationships, and the value of diverse writing activities, in her presentation of Patsy, "a very little girl, very tiny" but a child who could be a very large handful in the class. As Andrea explained, Patsy's diary revealed the child's conflicted feelings about both Andrea and her peers, and her worries about being treated fairly:

> **Andrea:** This is [Patsy's] diary. It really gave me insight . . . [about] some of the problems she's having in the classroom dealing with me personally. She thinks I'm on the girls all the time, and not on the boys. I value the diaries. . . . That was one of the purposes, so I could see if they were having any problems or experiences that they can't cope with. . . . They pull them out all day long and write in them.

On the other hand, story writing displayed not only Patsy's compositional skills but also her thoughtfulness about how people feel and act, and about issues of gender and race—a thoughtfulness not always evident in Patsy's public behavior in the real world, where a tough stance seemed important to her.

> **Andrea:** She'll sit over in the corner and write. If you say write anything, she'll sit there and she will write. . . . This is about best friends. It sounds like it's about a Black girl and a white girl in here. [Patsy, who is Black, is writing from the perspective of the white girl.] "There was a girl and her name was Sandy, and she was walking with one of her friends and her friend's name was Andy. And she always played with her. But one day she went over to her house and she did not see no one there. 'I wonder where she could be? I hope nothing bad happened to her because she is my best friend.' So Sandy went on home and laid on her bed and she was thinking

about where Andy could be. Then Sandy went to go over Andy's house again. . . . [Andy] was sitting on the couch and her mother and father both had their fingers in her face and she heard them say, 'You better not play with a white girl.' And so Sandy thought to herself and said, 'What's wrong with playing with a white person? I am nice to her. I let her play with my toys sometimes. She even has supper with us.'. . . [After Sandy's and Andy's parents talk things over] they all hugged and shook each other's hands. . . . And so Andy and Sandy shook hands and went outside."

Judi: This girl can write!

And that writing, like the writing and dictating of many other children, gave us insights into relationships Patsy reflected about and enacted.

Summary: *"What Are You?"*

"What are you?" the pen pal asked James, a question James understood but resisted. As our stories suggested, it is uncomfortable to find ourselves, at any age, reduced to someone else's label, but it is also uncomfortable to find important aspects of our lives, especially relationships with family and friends, denied or left out of the common world represented in classroom texts and talk.

FIGURE 11 | JUDI'S CHILDREN: THE WORLD IN FORMATION.

Thus, we considered our experiences as teachers who foster and monitor relationships between and among ourselves and our students. As a group, we placed great value on community activities and on *individual participation in and contribution to those joint activities.* We did not always find this inclusion easy—and it is possible, as the child Maxine noted, for teachers to "scare the voice away." But through manipulation of social structures (be they working partners, classroom stages, or private coaching), through verbally monitoring group dynamics and marking individual response, we worked to support children's sense that they were competent, valued participants in the classroom whole.

At the same time, opening up curricular space for children's contributions brought their diverse present worlds and their family and cultural heritages into that space. *Common texts both formed from and chosen to reflect that diversity* could yield common discussions, in which we could support children's efforts to develop *thoughtful and critical stances toward texts;* such stances are necessary if children are to participate in and help transform their world. At the same time, private texts, like diaries, interpersonal ones, like letters and memos, and individually authored ones, like essays and stories, were also *written means for revealing and helping children negotiate the complex interpersonal relations* of any community life.

Thus, we worked against the sort of classroom misery Hong Kingston felt, awkwardly aware of her own "difference" and of her own failure to meet the rigid expectations of her teacher. And we worked toward curricular substance, interactional space, and literacy tools that would allow each child some agency in defining his or her valued place in the community as a whole.

Issues We Reflect On

1. **What is "a classroom community"?**

   a. What evidence exists in your classroom site that a classroom community is developing?

   b. What is the relationship between developing a classroom community and developing literacy? How do teachers negotiate vertical and horizontal differences among children in fostering this relationship?

2. **How is trust built between and among teachers and children?**

   a. How do teachers learn about their children's perceptions of them?

b. To what extent does sharing sociocultural common ground with children—for example, being of the same race, speaking the same first language, belonging to the same cultural community—contribute to a feeling of trust? How can trust be built without such common ground?

c. How have cultural differences (i.e., differences in ways of interpreting, and of communicating about, experiences) figured into your relationships with students? into students' relationships with each other? How are such differences recognized and incorporated?

3. **How does the study of sociocultural differences help children become aware of themselves and their world?**

a. How should race, class, and gender figure into the school literacy curriculum for primary grade children (K–3)?

b. How should teachers address linguistic and sociocultural differences that exist in our society but not in their own classrooms?

Resource Sampler

Derman-Sparks, L., & the Anti-Bias Curriculum Task Force. (1989). *Anti-bias curriculum: Tools for empowering young children.* Washington, DC: National Association for the Education of Young Children.

> A practical book that offers sound guidance and useful resources for teachers seeking to interact with young children in ways that help them develop as confident, empathetic people able to speak up for themselves and others.

Genishi, C., Dyson, A. H., & Fassler, R. Z. (1994). Language and diversity in early childhood: Whose voices are appropriate? In B. Mallory & R. S. New (Eds.), *Diversity and developmentally appropriate practices* (pp. 250–268). New York: Teachers College Press.

> By presenting teachers and children interacting in three educationally different settings, the authors consider the nature of classroom communities that incorporate

culturally and linguistically diverse voices. The school whose 1970s beginnings are discussed by Genishi is the same school site discussed by Judi Garcia in this monograph.

Harris, V. J. (Ed.). (1992). *Teaching multicultural literature in grades K–8.* Norwood, MA: Christopher-Gordon Publishers.

> An information-packed volume on children's literature written by people of color. The chapters offer wonderful lists of recommended children's books.

Ladson-Billings, G. (1994). *The dreamkeepers: Successful teachers of African American children.* San Francisco: Jossey-Bass.

> Inspiring portraits of successful teachers of African American children, all teachers whose classrooms are intellectually challenging and culturally relevant. Ladson-Billings addresses directly the issue of trusting relationships between teachers and children who may or may not share a common cultural identity.

Levine, D., Lowe, R., Peterson, B., & Tenorio, R. (Eds.). (1995). *Rethinking schools: An agenda for change.* New York: The New Press.

> This volume is full of thought-provoking articles, most taken from *Rethinking Schools: An Urban Educational Journal*—a quarterly journal grounded in both realities of urban classrooms and policy issues of social justice and equity. Much attention is paid to all aspects of the language arts curriculum. The journal's address is 1001 E. Keefe Ave., Milwaukee, WI 53212.

Nieto, S. (1992). *Affirming diversity: The sociopolitical context of multicultural education.* New York: Longman.

> An exploration of the complex interplay of personal, linguistic, social, political, and educational factors that yield educational success or failure for our diverse student population. Nieto includes ten rich case studies of adolescents, who allow insight into the interplay of these factors as they have experienced them in their relations with teachers and peers throughout their school years.

Paley, V. G. (1989). *White teacher.* Cambridge, MA: Harvard University Press.

> Like all Vivian Paley's books, this one brings readers into the worldview of a master teacher who pays close attention to her children's perceptions of her, each other, and themselves; through this attention—and with the interactive support of an African American colleague—Paley learns to respond more openly to issues of racial differences. Readers may also be interested in her 1995 book on this topic, one based on her dialogues with parents and colleagues as well as children: *Kwanzaa and Me: A Teacher's Story* (Cambridge, MA: Harvard University Press).

Chapter 4 | Negotiating Permeable Activities

"At First I Didn't Understand"

Walking down Fifth Avenue in New York not long ago, I came up behind a couple and their young son. The child, about four or five years old, had evidently been complaining about big dogs. The mother was saying, "But why are you afraid of big dogs?" "Because they're big," he responded with eminent good sense. . . . "But there's really no difference [between big dogs and little dogs]," said the mother, pointing to a large slathering wolfhound with narrow eyes and the calculated amble of a gangster, and then to a beribboned Pekinese the size of a roller skate, who was flouncing along just ahead of us. . . . "See?" said the father. "If you look really closely you'll see there's no difference at all. They're all just dogs."

P. Williams, *The Alchemy of Race and Rights*

Legal scholar Patricia Williams marvels at the power of language—not only to capture the diversity of human experience (as she does in her own prose)—but to squeeze out that experience, to reduce diversity to a single truth: "They're all just dogs." That truth, Williams points out, tends to issue forth from those comfortably in charge of saying how the world works; in the above case, it issues forth from adults who, in the process, "obliterate" their child's viewpoint, "to say nothing of [that of] . . . the slathering wolfhound, from whose own narrow perspective I dare say the little boy must have looked exactly like a lamb chop" (p. 13).

In discussions of our school lives with children, we grappled with the complexities of understanding children's worldviews and, more particularly, with making classroom activities permeable, open to children's language and experiences. Such permeability was not so much planned as negotiated in the moment, as sometimes-baffled adults worked to understand child sense. Moreover, permeability raised its own sort of tensions, as our talk often revealed: the challenge was both to tap child sense and, then, to figure out how to respond to it. Listen, for example, to this exchange between Linda and Louise:

Linda: But I just think that's really powerful, that if kids are allowed to sort of play out what's going on in their lives, and then through that—you know the little Power Rangers [a media cartoon very popular among young school children]? That's what's important to them, that's what they're interested in. . . . They use all those things to learn with. . . .

Louise: And somehow that it has to be the role of the teacher to know how to extend it, to take the stuff that's important to the kid. Because you don't want them just reliving their past. There has to be a way of extending.

The negotiated nature of a "permeable curriculum" (Dyson, 1993)—its emergent quality, its valuing of "what's important to them" and, also, its way of "extending" children's worlds—was captured in a story Carolyn told about two of her first graders, Kathy and Amy:

Carolyn: [There's] two little girls in the classroom, one named Kathy and the other one named Amy. . . . [Kathy] had this book, *Anna Banana* [Cole, 1989]—it's the jump-rope rhymes. I think I told you about that, about how they [copy] rhymes out of it. Well, Kathy did her own rhyme and apparently at home she spoke it into a tape recorder and when she came to school she taught it to Amy. And previous to that Amy knew a song that she had at home and she had [taped it and] taught it to the class. So Kathy taped her poem . . . and then she came to school, and she was telling Amy about it. . . . Well when Amy came to share her journal that day she had written the poem that Kathy had taught her. And she got up and she said it for the class. . . . She tells it just like Kathy. And Amy is white and Kathy is Black. . . . At first I couldn't understand it. . . . Amy really uses . . . [invented] spelling a lot. . . . But . . . she had all of the elements of Kathy's intonation: the tone, just the dialect— everything—in it. . . .

Louise: Did Kathy mind that it showed up in Amy's writing?

Carolyn: No, and it's really interesting, because Kathy—when she first came in in September, she cried like the first fifteen minutes every day. She really had a hard time separating from mom and becoming a part of the classroom. She's very shy. . . . So she's really sort of coming out and just the fact that she . . . created this poem and she told it to Amy and she's sharing herself. It's a big step, because she's been very withdrawn. . . .

Following are edited and unedited versions of Amy's written rendition of Kathy's poem:

EEK! Shut up stairs!	EEC sap sdar
Get on my darn nerves.	gto my dn nrs
EEK! Shut up stairs!	EEC sap sdar
Get on my darn nerves.	gto my dn nrs
Yep.	YAP
Just like my lil' Lizabeth.	jt lc my lto Lesab
She eat <u>dirt</u>. She eat <u>buuugs</u>.	se et drt se et bacs

When Anne visited, Kathy and Amy performed the poem and then explained the poem's sense:

Anne: Who is Lizabeth?

Kathy: My friend.

Anne: She eats <u>dirt</u>? She eats <u>buuugs</u>?!?

Kathy: Well, I was just making that up. It's like, there's an adult saying that. Because when it goes: "EEEEK!" That means [Lizabeth] has a loud guitar. . . . Because she's upstairs and the adult says, "She get on my nerves." . . . And Lizabeth doesn't say nothing, but the adult keeps saying things and things. . . . And the adult's sister is over, and then she's talking to her sister, and she tells her about, "She eat dirt and she eat bugs."

Amy: Because she really hates her because of her guitar.

Amy's brief text—especially in its unedited form—does not seem to make much sense. But, out of the unfolding story of classroom relationships and of literacy learning came a found poem, so to speak.

The stuff of that poem, so appealing to both Kathy and Amy, was the poetry of a scene that could be looked at differently—a scene of mother/daughter tension and frustrated words. But Kathy captured the poetry of everyday language and the humor of a family dialogue, an exchange between a silent child and outspoken adults brought together by a loud guitar. In so doing, Kathy also captured the attention of another playful language-lover, Amy, who explored the pleasures of new language rhythms.

FIGURE 12 | Performing an original poem in Carolyn's room.

Kathy's and Amy's shared poem was steeped in child experience and language, shaped in a classroom that valued child play, and shared yet again in a group of teachers whose sense of classroom joy came from such language puzzles and child surprises, the sorts of things one didn't "at first understand." In the interrelated sections ahead, we examine in more detail both the possibilities and the challenges of the permeable curriculum and, more particularly, of writing activities. We consider the qualities of activities that allow us to perceive and negotiate with children's diverse resources and needs.

We first discuss how variation in children's literacy knowledge and know-how pushed against the edges of our planned activities and moved us to offer activities that *allow space for diverse sorts of child participation.* In our case studies, however, child agency and decision making was linked to teacher agency and decision making. Tapping the diversity of children's resources was more complex than simply providing paper, pencils, and time to write.

In our second section, we discuss our sense that certain children seemed adrift in the very space that allowed others to thrive. In our narratives, we referred to activities that could *provide children with familiar curricular content and familiar oral genres* (or ways of using language) to couch or provide a guiding context for new writing efforts.

Finally, in the third section, we discuss our sometimes ambivalent feelings about the experiential resources available in children's worlds and, thus, brought to the classroom. We valued activities that *help children bring diverse perspectives to bear on their familiar worlds*, that is, that help them imagine and reimagine varied ways of being.

Throughout the chapter, our stories of children illustrate the ongoing negotiation of teaching. In our classrooms, we aimed both to open up activities to child resources and invention *and* to ease children's way toward new possibilities. This sort of negotiation was most visible— and teaching seemed both rewarding and challenging—when activities allowed us access to the puzzles and surprises of children's worlds.

Letting Go and Making Choices: Linking Teacher and Child Options

"I had to let go some of the strategies that I have used previously," said Carolyn one night. "I was frustrating myself." And she went on to locate her frustration in narrow expectations for child participation in early composing.

Carolyn: I'd give these lists of words [to my first graders], and they'd have *thing* and *that* and *the,* and they'd have the test on Friday. And then Monday they'd be writing in their journals and ask, "How do you spell *thing*?" One time a kid said [that] to me. I said that it was the spelling word from last week, and [he] said, "Oh, is that the same one?" You know, there was no connection between it. . . . That was the only method that they had for getting words on paper, to use the spelling list and what I had up in the room.

So when I became a little bit more open and said, "You can write it anyway that you want to, and you can scribble it [or dictate it]. It can be a drawing—words *and* pictures." When I opened up my notion of what literacy was about, then I think it really changed my style in terms of expectation of what kids in my room would do. . . . My goal now is to get kids to enjoy writing and reading. . . . I try not to stifle them at all. . . . I let them work [problems] out. Some kids will come to me and say, "Is this the front, or is *this* the front [of my writing book]?" And then I'll say, "Let's open it up, here's how you can tell.". . . So allowing kids to experiment. . . .

I've played with language a lot with them. Before we go to lunch I have them look at the alphabet. . . . We did the beginning letter [sounds] at the beginning of the year, now [we do the end sounds]. . . . Sometimes they say, "We don't know what that sounds like," and I say, "I don't either." Then they start to say, "Maybe that's it." And we play with the words. I think that they know that they have this license to play with language, and that whatever they put down is acceptable. In the beginning stages, to me, that's important. I feel like kids have to be able to do that in order for me to be able to teach them how to spell. We need to have something down on paper for them to write.

In Carolyn's reflections on her changing ways of teaching, she refers both to her efforts to make space for different ways in which children might begin to write in school and, also, to her ways of helping children enter and exploit that provided space. In Carolyn's experience, child agency was linked to teacher agency, to enacting a playful, experimental stance toward language and learning that invited child participation.

Indeed, the complex link between teacher agency and child agency undergirded many of our discussions about child writing. As Carolyn told her children, there are various options for composing on paper. But those options draw on different sorts of child resources, and they serve potentially different instructional outcomes. There is only limited time to spend with each child, and taking one action to open up a new possibility for child participation may, at the same time, close off another possible route.

For example, particularly with the youngest child writers, we referred often to negotiating the tension between wanting children to communicate their ideas on paper through any means possible, on the one hand, and helping them develop new strategies, like inventing a spelling, on the other. The two discussion excerpts below capture these negotiations. In the first, Linda has been talking about Lisa, who enjoys making books—filling child-stapled pages or teacher-constructed journals with pictures and letters and letter-like shapes. Once, when Linda asked Lisa to explain her page to her, Lisa started telling a story and, at the same time, adding more letters:

Linda: She writes all over [the page, including writing over what she has already written]. . . .

Judy: She was editing her own work.

Jill: Revising.

Judy: Yes, sometimes they imitate adult behavior. She was going back and fixing it. . . .

Louise: You know, although she doesn't have sound/symbol, she does have word relationships. She knows that she is saying something. Something is coming out and something should be down. . . . I find that kids when they get to this stage . . . sometimes I sort of push them into labeling. I would say to her, "Is this the bear [in your story]?" Then, if she says yes, I would say, "Bear. I wonder if you can write the word *bear*. . . ."

During composing time, then, we might support children in their exploration of writing process and forms, helping them more systematically match letters and sounds. On other occasions, we might be drawn into (and draw a child into) an extended conversation, trying to understand a child's worldview and, moreover, to develop talk itself. On still other occasions, we might help a child develop a kind of text or genre, for example, a story or a letter:

Linda: I used to do journals where I would try to get them to say one sentence [after they had finished their own drawing and writing]. Then I could write it down, and I could get them to read this back [a helpful strategy for supporting children's early reading]. Then I felt like I wasn't getting their language out. . . . And since I [stopped doing that] I've really noticed that Lisa's stories started changing. Her last story made a lot more sense. It had a beginning, a middle, and an end.

Louise: One of the issues that I have to deal with is the question of dictation. One of my students had come back [from our field trip to the fire station] and was absolutely certain that she was going to be a firefighter. She was using her beautiful language to discuss this. So I then had to decide if I was going to do dictation or to sit there doing beginning and ending sounds. I just decided that if I didn't take dictation then it was gone. So I did, and I took this incredible dictation. I know that there are people who don't feel that you should take dictation.

Judi: I disagree with those people.

Louise: I think you need both.

As a group we disagreed with any rigid pronouncements about what teachers should or should not do. We, like our children, needed negotiating space for exploring and exploiting diverse possibilities for our children in any particular moment.

In fact, from our very first meeting, we referred to activities in which both students and teachers could participate in varied ways. As Andrea put it, "When you teach the curriculum [so that] . . . everything is an activity. . . . That's where you see the growth; the next year, kids can expand on the same activities"—and so can the teacher.

For example, when Jill presented Shane she talked about the kinds of decisions he had made within the context of particular activities, decisions about text substance and style, print format and arrangement, even about writing partner and writing time. However, as Jill talked, the rest of us continually questioned her about what *she* was doing:

Jill is discussing how Shane and his peer Brent engaged in the writing aspect of the Frog and Toad activity, which involved multiple drafts of a composed story followed by the making of puppets and the performance.

Jill: Shane and Brent had a hard time writing together because they would fight a lot about what they wanted to write. Both agreed on the ideas, but they fought about spelling. It was interesting to see how they went about this. . . . Even though [Shane] doesn't have very good [knowledge of] sound/symbol relationship, he has a better [grasp of] sound/symbol relationship than Brent does. But Brent seems to have higher status than Shane. [Brent was getting his way.] Then when we got toward the end [of writing this draft] I said to Brent, . . . "You have to trust one another, and you'll have to listen to one another when you sound out words for spelling."

Kristin: Is there any intervention [between drafts]? Do you talk to them about their stories in between?

Jill: I will talk to them, and they will read it to me, and I'll ask them where they are going with it, if they've made some changes. It's not only me that does that. Sometimes there are children who are finished or are working on something else and there is peer tutoring going on. In fact on the next piece, the research piece after the Frog and Toad story—

Judi: Which [text] is quite wonderful because they caught the spirit of the story. (In the boys' story, Toad made Frog a bug sandwich— but the bug jumped out and Toad caught it with his tongue. "I thought you made the sandwich for me," said Frog.)

Jill: Yes, even with the Frog and Toad story, we talk about anthropomorphism, where authors can make animals talk, but that's not true with living things. We can talk about how you can mix fact and fiction. They did introduce the bug into the sandwich, and frogs and toads eat insects. . . .

To get into the dialogue, one pretends they are Frog and one pretends they are Toad, and that's how a lot of them come up with their dialogue. They have a great time doing that.

Louise: Did you do the corrections?

Jill: Absolutely not. That's how they come along, and now they are learning how to use the format [function on the computer for revising]. They use cut and paste.

Carolyn: Then [in the next draft] they started to double space.

Jill: I said there is a storyteller, a frog, and a toad, so you've got your dialogue. What they went to was the book to see what the publisher did there and separated the dialogue. We had all decided that's how they wanted to do it. It would be easier to read for them and it would look more like a published story. That's what they wanted to do.

Then I said, "OK, you have to read each part and you have to determine if it's the storyteller telling the part or the frog having dialogue or the toad having dialogue. Everything is going to be separated." So they went and read it to each other and decided where they were going to separate it. That's what they did on that.

Louise: Do they use spell check?

Jill: No they do not. I don't let them. . . . I will sit with them, or I'll have someone else sit with them and they go through. We'll read and I'll say, "What do you think about this sentence?". . .

Anne: How did you decide who would work with each other?

Jill: I actually let them choose their writing partners in the beginning. I didn't want to intervene on that. I would have never put those two together but they chose one another, so I let it be.

Anne: How do they plan their time to write?

Jill: They have to decide that. . . . I tell them to look at the clock to determine how much time they have. There's isn't much squabble over the time. . . . [I say], "Talk about it. How can you do this? Does everybody want to type? Make sure everybody is included."

A single activity can involve diverse means of participation, among them oral conversation and literary language, spelling and content planning, book consulting and time telling, formatting and social negotiating, drawing and dramatizing. "You have to decide," said Jill, making space for child agency, but she was deciding too, deciding to focus their attention on one aspect of the task or another, to make, or not make, a certain demand, and both child and teacher agency were situated within a well-understood and appealing task—composing puppet plays about Frog and Toad. It may be just this child agency that contributed to Shane's declaration, earlier quoted, that he was, after all, "a good learner."

"Go Right Back and Write Every Word": On "Freeing" the Children to Write

"I just don't feel I'm moving along too well with this journal writing," said Elise one fall night. "It's a little frustrating. . . . I was trying to be freer about it and just have them put in whatever they felt like. . . . And yet I gave them a theme for [this entry] because they seemed so lost. They didn't understand the concept of the journal."

Elise felt she had an unusually quiet class this year (although, as we mentioned, by midwinter, that "unusually quiet class" had quite disappeared!). The children, twenty-nine in all, did not seem to be "chatty," even with each other: "They don't call each other anything right now. . . . They don't use names with each other. They work in isolation." And (as we also mentioned) she had few native English speakers; most of her children had heritages rooted in different Asian countries.

FIGURE 13 | Concentrating hard in Elise's room.

Her children did enjoy drawing in their journals—and she delighted in detailed pictures of ninja turtles, pumpkins, and pigs, to name a few of the dominant topics. But Elise did not feel the connection to "making up a story" was clear, and most attempts at writing were carefully spelled English words copied from the environment.

Elise's challenges move us further into these complex issues of teacher and child agency. Our narratives of children did reveal the link we made between diversity of child resources and openness of school activities. But they also suggested that we felt some children were unsure of the sense of an activity, of the worth of their own resources, and, for these children, a wide open landscape of possibilities—like "draw and write whatever or however you want"—could seem a scary void.

We consistently responded to children we judged hesitant, confused, or even "scared to death," in Elise's words, with a more deliberate anchoring of activities in familiar ground; with such anchoring we hoped to build firm, supportive structures for children to lean on. These supportive structures could be built, in part, with themes and stories from the common class curriculum, to echo the themes of Chapter 3.

Elise in fact was doing just that (establishing supportive structures), but sometimes, in the fall of the year, it's hard to see that, yes, the community is forming, literacy is finding roots there. Like all of us, Elise worked to interweave literacy itself throughout the children's day. For example, a class study of favorite foods might involve collectively reading recipes, listing ingredients, or composing charts of "what we love to eat." And Elise also made much use of stories, chants, and songs, which she would translate into Chinese for her students. Symbols of these appealing school experiences—as well as common experiences outside of school— were winding their way into the children's efforts, as these young school entrants began to explore, and to play, within the journal activity.

Their copied words and drawn pictures were symbols of shared experiences, rooted in popular culture (e.g., ninja turtles, Santa Claus, and Mickey Mouse), school study units (e.g., admonitions to "Brush your teeth"), and children's rhymes and stories (e.g., *The Three Little Pigs,* "Five Little Pumpkins [sitting in a row]"). These symbols appeared amidst the recurrent child renditions of houses and rainbows—and, for one little fellow, pages and pages of balloons. As children observed each other's efforts, themes spread like ivy among the children.

Indeed, our youngest children sometimes made unexpected connections between curricular phenomena, especially early in the year. Surrounded by a wealth of new experiences, new language, and new symbols, they intermingled the new with the old in ways that could seem jarring to adults. In this, our children were similar to those described by many observers of the young, including master teacher Vivian Paley (e.g., 1986), developmental psychologist Catherine Garvey (1990), and child folklorists Peter and Iona Opie (1959). For example, listen to Judi explain a drawing and its accompanying dictation by Anita, one of her focal children; like other young children, Anita seemed to be mainly naming the objects in her picture, but putting those names or labels within a familiar "once-upon-a-time" story frame:

Judi: (reading Anita's dictation) "Un día había un árbol de Merry Christmas." One day there was a Merry Christmas tree. "Y venían los estars." And the stars came. *Estar*. In Spanish it is *estrellita*. The *es* is very common [for Spanish-speakers learning English]. . . . "Y venía una mariposa. . . ." That means, there came a butterfly . . . and a bear and a monkey. Now this is coming in because we've . . . been separating the farm animals from the animals in the jungle. "Y ví un ratoncito." And I saw a little mouse. That could have been because the kids knew we had to have an exterminator come in.

In a single piece, Anita had textual allusions to many key classroom themes in the late fall.

In addition to thematic supports, we also referred often to familiar ways of using language or, to use more formal words, familiar oral genres that could be used as a context for written genres. For example, we have referred already to Carolyn's interview activity, in which children readily adopted the role of the note-taking interviewer (and understood the role of the interviewee), and to Jill's oral puppet play, in which child composers acted out a dialogue between characters, dialogue that could be written down. Other activities that couched child writing in familiar oral language use were Kristin's Author's Theater and, not previously mentioned, Louise's class video library of dramatized fairy tales (made by taping over promotapes given away by Blockbuster Video).

We also referred to conversation itself, to our one-to-one interactions with children whose personal and school histories seemed to have left them with little confidence in their academic selves. Both Andrea and Carol talked about how much support and direction it could take to "free" such children to write. In their experience, the children seemed to need an oral response to each planned written sentence; supporting the children's writing was similar to holding a conversation, one that ended with a directive to "write that down."

Andrea, for example, discussed her student Carl:

Andrea: In the beginning Carl did very little writing. He hardly did anything. He just sat. . . . And what I found out was the hardest thing for the children to do [in writing about books they had read], if they could tell me what happened, but they couldn't put it in writing. So I would say, "tell me again." And he would tell me, and I'd say, "OK, go right back to your seat and write down every word that you can remember that you told me." Because that was the hardest thing for them to do. . . .

Carol talked about her student Allen's hesitation about writing. When she discussed possible writing ideas with him, Allen would end each sentence with a questioning intonation, as if asking, "Is it OK to say that?" On their visit to Carol's room, Elizabeth and Anne observed the patience both Carol and Allen brought to their interactions:

Carol has been working through Allen's composition with him, one he initiated about school friends. They are concentrating on his last sentence: "One day Philip got off the bus and walked to school a friend named Fred whose sister named Veronica."

Carol: Did he walk to school *with* Fred and his sister?

Allen: Yup.

Carol: OK, so we need to add a word that lets us know that he walked *with*, "He got off the bus and walked to school (pause)

Allen: *with*

Carol: with Fred

Allen: and his sister named Veronica.

Carol: Does that make sense if we just put *with* there? . . . How does that sound?

Allen: Very fine.

As Carol is helping Allen figure out how to spell with, *another child comes up to get Carol's help. The child is having difficulty figuring out what to write. Allen pipes up with a suggestion for the frustrated child:*

Allen: Oh, you took it down, the list of all the things that you can write.

Carol:	What did I take down?
Allen:	You know, the list of all the stuff we could write.
Carol:	Oh, I did! To give her some ideas. You're right! I did take it down. So I need to put that back up. You're right, I'm going to put that back up. OK, so let's keep going. . . . Is there a problem that comes up? Because, remember we talked about most stories have a problem? What's going to be the problem?
Allen:	Yup, problem. They're going to get into a fight.

Carol:	What were they fighting over?
Allen:	I haven't thought of that yet.

Carol persists and Allen comes up with an idea.

Allen:	Sashiko passed the test.

Carol helps Allen figure out how to write that, and then asks "So she passed the test, why does Ashley want to fight her?"

Allen:	And Sashiko asked, "How did you do?" And Ashley said that she didn't pass the test. And Ashley thought that Sashiko was teasing her, but she wasn't.
Carol:	OK. AH! That's the reason why they fought. So let's make one more sentence before—it's almost time for lunch.

Within the structure of a supportive conversation, Allen was able not only to write but also to reveal his insight about the social world of school and his attentiveness to the working of the classroom community—including the helpful list of potential topics. For Allen, as for other children, shared experiences and interactive oral activities (with teachers and peers) were supportive structures, kinds of "scaffolding," to use a term inspired by Russian psychologist Lev Vygotsky (Cazden, 1988); in our view, these structures could ease children into written ways of expressing themselves, exploring ideas, and communicating with, and performing for, others. Deciding what's supportive and what's stifling, what's "giving a necessary push" and what's stopping important "playing with language" is part of the daily work of teaching, work guided by our knowledge of each child—and by our willingness to be surprised.

Appropriating, Playing, and Censoring: On Reimagining the World

On their visit to Linda's room, Wanda and Anne watched Lisa hard at work at the writing table. What exactly she was doing was certainly a puzzle, but she did seem to have a plan. Lisa was concentrating hard on cutting out rectangular pieces of paper, writing numbers on them, and then pasting two pieces back to back. And indeed, Lisa did have a plan. She was, she told an inquiring Anne, making a deck of cards for her Grandma. Her Grandma liked to play cards with her friends. And Lisa watched them. She played cards too—"but not with my grandma's cards."

Watching Grandma play cards with her friends—this is an example of the experiential stuff, the activities that make up Lisa's everyday life. And her constructed deck of cards is an example of the symbols that help her bring her home life into the new world of school. Lisa was, in a sense, replaying experiences by making use of her emerging literacy skills— just as she had done earlier in the day, when she read and reread her dictation for the class "Morning News Book": "My Grandma is taking me to Disneyland." In Linda's words, "Everything she was doing related to what was going on in her life."

As already suggested, we placed great value on children playing and replaying with their family and community experiences in school through the new tools of reading and writing. Indeed, this is what Kathy and Amy were doing collaboratively in the opening anecdote. Kathy's representation of an everyday scene emerged, first, in an oral form and, then, in a written one; and both she and Amy seemed inspired by a new experience—by finding a book in which oral rhymes took shape in written form. Carolyn had, in fact, first brought up Kathy's fascination with the jump-rope rhyme book a month before she told about her poem:

Carolyn: We had RIF (Reading Is Fundamental) a few weeks ago, and one of the books that they really liked was *Anna Banana* [Cole, 1989], which has a lot of jump-roping rhymes in it. So this kid got up to read her journal yesterday—Kathy, and I looked over, and it said, "I won't go to Macy's anymore." And I thought, "What happened at Macy's?" And then she got up to read it, and it's a jump-rope rhyme. She had copied it from her book.

Anne: Is that the [rhyme] where there's a "Big, Fat" something?

Carolyn: Yes, "There's a big, fat policeman at the door, door, door."

Anne: [Kristin's student] Makeda's got [a jump-rope rhyme that I heard when I observed at her school]:
"I ain't going to school no more more more.
There's a big, fat kid at the door door door.
He grabbed me by the collar,
and asked me for a dollar.
I ain't going to school no more more more."

Carolyn: And you know, that's what happened. That's exactly what we did. She wrote it and copied it out of the book. And I said, "Why did you copy it?" And she said, "I think it's funny, and I like it." And I said, "That's great.". . . And she said, "You know where I got it from?. . . The *Anna Banana* book." And I said, "Oh that's great." So she read it.

And I said, "You know, boys and girls, could we change this poem?" And I thought of that, because if she liked it, she can also make it her own by doing what you just did. So we did our own. Somebody said we could change it to pennies. And then we changed it from a dollar to fifty cents. I mean we just kind of played around with it a little bit and had fun. So they went out the door to lunch singing, "I won't go to Chucky Cheese [a pizza place] anymore more more." It just came to be this little game.

This sort of playfulness, this ability to turn around language—and the worlds represented in language—was mentioned again and again in our talk. Sometimes the emphasis was on play as children's way of taking control of the language and the symbols around them, making them their own by playing with them. This was an aspect of our first two chapter sections. However, such play with alternative versions of language and stories could also be a child-appropriate way of approaching complex issues of diversity.

For example, there were interesting differences in language between Makeda's rhyme, which came directly from the playground, and Kathy's, which came most immediately from a book. Just to illustrate, Makeda declared that she "ain't" going to do what Kathy "won't," so to speak. Makeda's rhyme—like Kathy's own poem—used nonstandard English (that is, a variation of the language that is different from that found in textbooks).

Nonstandard forms of English are examples of "horizontal" differences, differences that indicate nothing about children's intelligence and learning ability. But they also are differences that can be viewed as vertical differences—differences in level of language competence—by unknowledgeable others (a serious problem for teacher education, one discussed by Delpit, 1990, and Scott, 1990, among others). Standard and nonstandard forms of English were not, in fact, issues in our group. As teachers of young children, we were concerned that children make full use of their oral language(s) in entering into school learning and in beginning to read and write. We worried, as we have said over and over, about stifling the children, making them uncomfortable with their own voices.

Still, there was a great deal of play with different languages and different English dialects and styles in our stories. For example, Jill talked about how her children reread the Frog and Toad stories, trying to make their own written dialogue sound like that of the book. Linda, Judy, and Carolyn all mentioned children's dictating, copying, or writing the appealing language they'd heard in books. Elise discussed how her children loved the chants and songs she had posted on charts throughout her room, and how she taught them the English and Chinese versions.

Judi presented examples of her children's ability to code-switch or move between different languages, sometimes deliberately translating their own comments from one language to another; Judi's school also had a literary magazine in which, as readers may recall, "students wrote their own way of writing English." Everyone, in fact, told stories of children taking pleasure in the ability to play with—take control of—language, an ability that most certainly should help them continue to learn new styles, new ways with words.

In addition to this display of language diversity, the children's play with symbols could make visible complex issues of cultural diversity as well. For example, when Anne, Elizabeth, and another young teacher, Noelle Allen, visited Judy's classroom, they were struck by the religious symbols in the children's journals—for example, their drawings of churches and Virgin Marys, which reflected the importance of religion in the children's Mexican heritage. They also noted more contemporary symbols, like cars, romantic scenes, and names drawn block-style in "Cholo letters" (a handwriting style used to mark personal possessions and, sometimes, public property, especially by youth affiliated with gangs); these symbols reflected the importance of older siblings in children's lives and, also, the children's interest in the youth culture of those siblings.

These symbols, Judy said, "were part of the children's world" and appeared in many open or permeable spaces in her school day. For example, the children reported important cultural events, such as did the girls who anticipated gifts on the day of Our Lady of Guadalupe. They also used youth symbols to participate in classroom interviewing and graphing activities; for example, boys sometimes asked children to choose between two popular automobiles. (Indeed, cars were more popular topics than Power Rangers or other television superheroes in Judy's class.)

Sometimes, though, Judy negotiated with, rather than simply acknowledged or built on, the children's symbols. She was, for example, very concerned about the barely dressed women draped over cars in the *Lowrider* magazine some boys brought to school. Judy told the boys that "I'm a woman too, and I don't like to see pictures of women used like this." Judy did not allow the magazine in her classroom—but she did buy an alternative magazine *HotRodder,* which did not depict women in that way.

Judy's response to material that offended her, "I'm a woman too," was, in fact, a response many of us reported using when the children's work reflected aspects of our common culture that troubled us. And, as with the *Lowrider* magazine, those troubling aspects sometimes involved presentations of women and, in addition, visions of violence. Carolyn, for example, had a strong personal response to her children's stories for "Officer Wendy," the beat cop in her school's neighborhood.

Carolyn: Today, Officer Wendy, who is [the] cop on [our] avenue, came in . . . just to talk to them and answer questions. And then afterwards, because they . . . all wanted to talk, . . . [I] told them to go write . . . to Officer Wendy. Well what I got was a bunch of stuff about women, like shooting women, stabbing women. It was really disturbing. One kid I was sitting with, and taking dictation from, and I guess I might have shown something—either I cringed, or there was something in my body language that indicated it wasn't OK, because he said something like, "Then they shot the woman . . . But she got up anyway." . . . And then he looked at me, like, "Is that OK?" And I didn't know how far to go with it, because I want the stories to be theirs. . . . But I do have certain limits, in terms of they can't use things in the dramatic play center as guns. So I have things like that.

Jill: Then do they use their fingers?

Carolyn: They can't even use their fingers.

Linda: I have the same rule.

Judi: I'm so glad. That's great. Just think, if there are this many of us doing this, maybe we'll have an impact.

Carolyn: But I don't know if it's censoring their writing, or when I should step in and say, "No, she can't die," or "Why can't the woman do something to the man?"

We had, then, contradictory feelings about the permeable curriculum. We talked about opening our activities up to children's experiences and resources, but we were not always delighted with what the children brought in. Too, while we had rules about children's use of violence in their dramatic *play,* we did not have such rules about children's creative *writing,* their language play, so to speak. The value we placed on child ownership and language expression seemed to make problematic such rules, a dilemma also discussed by teacher-researcher Timothy Lensmire (1993).

And yet, we were all troubled by images of passive and helpless women and, moreover, by real and imagined worlds dominated by displays of physical power. Moreover, simply telling children that such images and such power are not valued could be like telling them that big dogs are not scary—a too easy dismissal of their own observations.

Kristin often offered her own classroom experience with these conflicts and issues. As we have mentioned, in her room, many boys wrote stories of superheroes, which they then acted out on the classroom stage. As did other group members, Kristin used play itself—and talk about play—to help children reflect on the kinds of characters and plots they were constructing. In her experience, children freely rewrote books they read, but—

Kristin: It seems harder to challenge them to take control of [media stories]. . . . I guess because there's a lot of status connected to [acting out those stories] in my class. But I agree that allowing them to [rewrite stories], or encouraging them to do that, is important. I'm still trying to free them. . . . We've been talking a lot about, "Does it have to be violent? Can you think of a different way for them to interact?. . ."

Carolyn: But it's kind of hard . . . if that's how [the Power Rangers] solve their problems is through fighting.

Kristin: That's what I mean. We're talking about Power Rangers [in my class] and how could the Power Rangers—or how could the X-Men [another set of superheroes] solve "the problem" without having to fight? Maybe we do [those alternative ways] in our own [classroom conflicts]. . . . "Why did they have to fight?" [I ask]. . . . "Because he's the bad guy," [they say]. "Why is he the bad guy? What did he do to be the bad guy?" "He was born a bad guy." So we had a talk about that. "Are people born bad guys?"

"I'm still trying to free them," said Kristin. Even when children are confident enough to take control of the act of writing, they are not necessarily "free" to write, she implied. "Free writing" isn't really free: children, like adults, may be controlled by accepted characters and plots that limit their imaginations, an argument made lately by many concerned with critical thinking in the language arts curriculum (e.g., Comber & O'Brien, 1993; Davies, 1989; Gilbert, 1994; Greene, 1988). One aspect of being free is being able to exploit the very strength of childhood, that is, the inclination to play, to turn the world on its head. Such play, as we have suggested throughout this chapter, is a way of exploring letters and sounds, story elements and language styles, imagined worlds and, by extension, the real worlds we are building together.

Summary: "At First I Didn't Understand"

Unlike the confidently didactic parents in Patricia Williams's anecdote, we had no illusions about our power as teachers and adults. We knew we could not simply explain how "the world" works to our children, nor could we explain their own views away. Indeed, for us, the fun and the struggles of teaching came from trying to understand what at first we often did not understand at all: *children's* interpretations of the world and the images and symbols it offered. Moreover, we valued children's sense of their own power to use language to participate in, and take some control of, the world around them.

Thus, we presented narratives of children deeply engaged in activities that *allowed for diverse means of participation;* through such participation, we felt, children could both experience and extend their powers as language users.

At the same time, however, the narratives also stressed our own deep involvement; in our view, children's sense of control was related to teachers' control, to our ability to make decisions that suit particular children's resources and nee oreover, our narratives featured activities that *provided children with the content and interactional support needed* to support

FIGURE 14 | Louise and children making a birthday book for their classmate Brandon (who loves spaceships and bugs) and going-away stories for their student teacher Sherry (who helped them a lot).

and guide children's ventures into written ways with words.

Our stories of children—and our questioning of each other—suggested that we thought a great deal about how to balance child and teacher agency. We valued activities that were open to children's free use of their own language, their own experiences, and their worlds of words. At the same time, however, our discussions suggested that freedom in language use does not only come from the absence of sanctions, but from the presence of imagination. Children may need help in seeing beyond the stories they are free to write, in imagining new possibilities. Thus, we were interested in activities that *brought diverse perspectives to bear on children's familiar words and worlds.*

It was with different perspectives on big dogs and loud guitars that we began this chapter. Throughout, we have aimed to make clear that opening up classroom activities to children's worlds is not an alternative to opening up children's worlds to new possibilities. Rather, these are interrelated aspects of our work as teachers, as mediators of sociocultural diversity, of the young and the old, of the present world and the future one we and the children will construct together.

Issues We Reflect On

1. **In your own experience, what are illustrative literacy activities that allow children to participate in many different ways? What qualities do those activities share?**

2. **How do educators "free" children to write?**

   a. Are there literacy activities in which you experience tension between making space for children's creativity and providing ample support and guidance?

b. In your own classroom, what sorts of familiar content and ways of using language have been useful supports for child writing?

c. Are there certain kinds of texts or genres your children have learned about mainly outside of school? Do your children know certain oral ways with words that differ from those considered "mainstream" (e.g., stories, jokes, songs, conversational skills)? How did you learn about those ways?

3. **What kind of play with language or story do your children enjoy? Have you been able to use that play to help them learn about linguistic and cultural diversity?**

4. **Should popular culture figure into language arts programs for young children? If so, how?**

a. Has popular culture been a positive force in your students' language and literacy learning? How?

b. Has it been a problematic force?

5. **What does "freedom of imagination" mean for the education of young children as writers?**

a. Are there themes, plots, or character portrayals in your own children's writing that have served as useful starting points for critical discussions?

b. Have children themselves ever initiated such discussions? If so, about what sorts of texts?

Resource Sampler

Cazden, C. (1992). *Whole language plus: Essays on literacy in the United States and New Zealand.* New York: Teachers College Press.

A thoughtful volume on how and why teachers negotiate literacy activities with children; Cazden discusses helping children both to manipulate details of language and print and to reflect on the larger societal contexts in which texts live.

Daiute, C. (1989). Play as thought: Thinking strategies of young writers. *Harvard Educational Review, 59,* 1–23.

Terrific examples of young children's playful strategies during collaborative composing; Jill's presentation of Katherine's and Ebony's oral play during writing (in Chapter 5) would be right at home in this piece.

Delpit, L. D. (1990). Language diversity and learning. In S. Hynds & D. L. Rubin (Eds.), *Perspectives on talk and learning* (pp. 247–266). Urbana, IL: National Council of Teachers of English.

A thought-provoking discussion of how teachers might help children appreciate our linguistic pluralism and gain access to a variety of language styles and dialects, including standard English. Delpit includes abundant examples, including many of young children exploring and exploiting language diversity.

Dyson, A. H. (1993). *Social worlds of children learning to write in an urban primary school.* New York: Teachers College Press. and Dyson, A. H. (in press). *Writing superheroes: The social and ideological dynamics of child writing.* New York: Teachers College Press.

Both of these publications are about creating permeable curricula that incorporate and extend the social intelligence, imagination, and linguistic and cultural resources of young children. The former project was completed in Louise's classroom, the latter in Kristin's.

Edelsky, C. (1994). Education for democracy. *Language Arts, 71,* 252–257.

An action-inspiring essay that speaks to both teachers' and children's freedom of imagination.

Mata, S., Trevino, B., Guzman, J., Roser, N., Hoffman, J., & Farest, C. (1991). Language learning from story (in three voices): Talking, reading, and writing in bilingual/ESL classrooms. In J. Feeley, D. Strickland, & S. B. Wepner (Eds.), *Process reading and writing: A literature-based approach* (pp. 217–228). New York: Teachers College Press.

Idea-generating examples of teachers and children playing with language, text, and story.

Chapter 5 | Portraits of Children Learning

"What Did You Think of Me?"

> I remember every teacher I ever had. . . . Some of them I knew quite well, particularly those in the elementary school, because of the intense relationship between elementary school teachers and their students in their self-contained classrooms and because they lived in my community. . . . Others I knew only as teachers. . . . Memories of the[se] others provoke a series of questions for me. Who were you really? What did you care about? What did you think of me? Did you even know who I was?
>
> **G. Ladson–Billings,** *The Dreamkeepers*

"What did you think of me?" asks the grown-up Gloria Ladson-Billings, reflecting back on her teachers. She did not wonder about those *she* knew well, those with whom she shared a sense of community in and out of the classroom. And those teachers were often elementary school teachers, who lived in her community. She wondered about those she did not know, those she knew "only as teachers." Undergirding her comments is the value elementary teachers have traditionally placed on knowing children as complex people, with memories and dreams, family stresses and cultural values, social pressures and personality quirks—as people in many ways just like their teachers. But it can be hard within the institution of the school to know children in these ways (and vice versa).

Throughout the previous chapters we have discussed how our own stories—our own visions—of students were shaped by the multiple dimensions of school life. As we discussed in Chapter 2, the child qualities we felt we must attend to, or "care about," were influenced by the ways our schools as institutions organized and categorized children. Within those structures, for example, our students could be "on-grade-level," "ahead," or "behind"; "bilingual," "ESL," or "English only"; a "behavioral problem," or "no-problem-at-all." These same categories influenced our relationships with parents and, indeed, with each other; we could become primarily partners who informed each other about unknown aspects of children's lives, past and present—or we could become mainly cautious evaluators who passed judgement on each other's competence.

The very fact that elementary teachers do spend many hours with many children in one small space also influenced the child qualities we attended to. As detailed in Chapter 3, we paid attention to individual children's relations with each other and with the classroom "community" as a whole. Children's shifting affiliations and social tensions, their contributions to common class projects, their varied responses to books and other media—all revealed both individual personalities and an evolving classroom community. Thus, we might, for example, describe a child as a "helper," "partner," "comforter," "teaser," "problem solver" or "problem causer," "nonstop talker," or "so quiet" that he or she disappeared in the crowd.

Both institutional structures (like being "a first grader," or an "English as a Second Language" child) and community relationships (like being a "partner," or a "problem solver") were realized in the context of the many activities that engaged both the children and us throughout the day. In Chapter 4 we illustrated how our knowledge about students was shaped by their ways of participating in those activities. Given our limited opportunities to know children outside the school walls, it was from that participation in activities that we learned about children's experiences in families, day care centers, and neighborhoods.

These institutional, relational, and activity dimensions of school life were the frames in which we learned about our children as complex individuals and as social and cultural beings. Those frames influenced whether and how we paid attention to sociocultural differences among children: differences could be framed as problems, resources, or simply "natural" variation in the human fabric.

In our narratives about children, these three dimensions were complexly intertwined, sometimes foregrounded, sometimes not, depending upon the interplay of contexts and personalities. In this chapter, we present fuller portraits of three of our children, aiming to illustrate this complex intertwining and, thereby, the complex nature of our narrated experiences. The portraits, all based on edited versions of the original oral presentations, feature Anita, Darian, and Katherine. These children differed in age, sex, ethnicity, language background, and family circumstance. And each portrait highlights different aspects of sociocultural difference. But all were presented by their teachers as starring characters in narratives about teaching, learning, and difference.

We frame each portrait with a brief description of the sociocultural variation present in the child's school as well as a description of the dominant concerns of the child's teacher about both curriculum and difference. Throughout each portrait are intertextual links with the themes of our earlier chapters, with, for example, our concerns about the interplay of language programs and ethnic diversity, about parent communication, curricular inclusion, and critical imagination. These thematic links exist because each portrait contributed to the development of the themes themselves and, thus, to our collective understandings about teaching and learning in city schools.

JUDI'S ANITA: BECOMING BILINGUAL

Judi's School and Classroom

A school district document reports that when Judi's school was "founded in 1975, it was temporarily housed in its present location"—which seems an apt description. The school consists primarily of a group of portable buildings on a lot near the city's central district. It has no playing field, no grassy expanse for children to run and play in, no large auditorium for all to gather together. What it has, however, is a strong history of attention to the needs of bilingual and bicultural children. Indeed, it began in response to parental pressure for a school that would help maintain their children's Spanish language and Chicano heritage. The district first offered a day care center and a kindergarten and, gradually, the school expanded to cover the elementary grades.

Over the years, the faculty has maintained this valuing of bilingualism and biculturalism. The population served by the school has changed, however. In the year of our project, only 53 percent of the school's children were Latino. And, although Judi's classroom had by tradition been a Spanish bilingual kindergarten, she had a diverse class: while the exact numbers varied during the year, she had roughly ten Latino children, ten Asian Americans (including both Vietnamese- and Chinese-speaking children), four African Americans, one European American, and one Eritrean American. As has historically been the case though, the majority of the children were from low-income homes (80 percent of the children qualified for the federal school lunch program).

During our project year Judi was a "Spanish bilingual teacher" with a multilingual and multicultural class. Moreover, her school and her district seemed caught in complex political struggles centered around a court-ordered consent decree—with one set of bilingual program requirements—and state law—with conflicting requirements. For Judi, then, the difference that made the most difference in her daily teaching experience was language. She was "conflicted," knowing that "if I don't [use Spanish] I'm cheating the children who speak Spanish, and if I do, what about the Asian children who speak Vietnamese or the Chinese children who are trying to learn English?"

Judi's response, in part, was to make beginning to learn about different languages a badge of inclusion in her class, something to be proud of. In addition, she was sensitive to children's growing command of English, as well as to the bilingual children's control of their native language; she herself made differential use of Spanish and English throughout the school day.

Further, like many teachers of children becoming bilingual (e.g., Enright, 1986; Genishi, Dubetz, & Focarino, in press), Judi stressed the importance of meaningful, concrete school experiences as a basis for language and literacy growth. "I teach thematically," she explained; "I have a [new] theme every four to six weeks. . . . I don't think kids can learn to read or write without being read to a lot, and without a chance for oral language development within a thematic context." Within that context, children drew and dictated contributions to a class book related to a theme, like her ongoing one about oceans. "I have all of the books we made last year; they are still in perfect condition. The kids treasure those books." In the sixth week of school, "we start keeping journals," using "magic writing; that means they can write whatever they want [and spell however they can]."

Given Judi's school and classroom context, it was sensible that language featured prominently in her presentation of Anita, a "bouncy little girl," a fluent speaker of Spanish, and a child beginning to learn English.

Anita's Portrait

"The child I chose [for our group]," began Judi one fall evening, "is Anita. She is in the bilingual day care center in the morning, and she comes to me in the afternoon. She is the sister of two boys that I also had. Their mother died of brain cancer during the time I had the boys. They really struggled in school. They were very quiet and nonparticipatory and had trouble just writing their names. But I couldn't tell how much of the boys' difficulties were [due] to their mother's death.

"Then when I found out that I was going to have Anita, I was curious if she was going to be similar to her brothers. Anita comes in, and I couldn't believe that she was their sister. This girl just talks all the time and has so much to say. In the tape I brought, she is talking [in Spanish] about her family. If you notice, she'll get confused if she's talking about her dead mom or the mom who lives now; the mother who lives now is from El Salvador, but her other mom was from Mexico. She talks about how she has a sister in El Salvador, but this is really the daughter of her mother now." On Judi's tape, Anita can be heard dictating a writing book entry about her family: Judi had overheard Anita telling her good friend Vanessa about her family, and Judi invited her to record her ideas; and so she did.

Anita: Yo crecí sola. [I grew up by myself.] Mi Mamá se murió. [My mom died.] Mis hermanos eran de México. [My brothers were from Mexico.] Mi hermana está en El Salvador solita. [My sister is by herself in El Salvador.] Está con la hermana de mi Mamá. [She is with my mom's sister.]

Like most people in the group, Judi had limited official allotted time for parent/child conferences. Still, she knew about Anita's family, in part, because of the informal, daily conversations she had with Anita's father during the years she had had Anita's brothers. Her knowledge of the family's native language made such conversation easier. Judi explained:

Judi: In kindergarten the parents drop the kids off. They're right there, and so I got to know him because I had one boy for two years and I had the other son. . . . We'd talk in the mornings when he'd bring [his children]. When his wife died I tried to express sympathy as best I could. It was so hard for him. Anita was a baby and he had to go back and forth to the hospital and try to get the boys to school on time.

Louise: Do they speak Spanish primarily at home?

Judi: Yeah. The father asked me . . . if Anita's speaking [that is, her talkativeness] bothered me, because he said at Centro [the day care] they complained. And they told him that sometimes they just have to say, "Anita, go away. Don't talk to me anymore." Because she is just always there telling you something.

Anne: Is that a problem when you teach?

Judi: Well, because there's an activity time when they can choose where they go. . . . That's when I really can talk to kids. . . . And that's when Anita always comes. She's just always so full of things to tell me. So I'm just trying to give you this image of her. She's this little girl who bounces around the room. She's always so happy and smiley.

Anita, this happy little girl, had been in the bilingual day care program during her preschool years, as, indeed, had other Latino children in Judi's class. Their history together seemed to increase children's comfort with each other, with their native language, and with being in school itself. On the other hand, it also meant that the group had "alliances and enemies" dating back to when they were in diapers together; thus Judi felt she had to help the group adjust to the more structured environment of the kindergarten and to the expectation that they would interact cooperatively with each other and the class as a whole. To this end, Judi planned small-group activities that mixed children dominant in different languages.

Judi felt Anita had become a good community member—and an unusually alert one. On the one hand, Anita had close friendships with Spanish-speaking children, and these friendships promoted the development of her Spanish and allowed the use of her stronger language for problem solving, extended conversations, and for talk about books and her own written texts with peers. On the other hand, Anita was also interested in and engaged with the class as a whole. Indeed, Judi made sure that Anita's attentiveness to the class community was viewed positively by our group:

Judy: [Anita's] not a meddler . . . ?

Judi: A little bit. You know, she's got to come tell me "and so-and-so is sitting in front of so-and-so but actually he got there after so-and-so." . . . But with Anita, it's not [like she is a meddler]. With her it's more like she's just kind of overseeing everything that's going on in the classroom and wants to be sure I am too.

Judy: Is she like a caretaker?

Jill: It sounds like it.

In fact, when Elizabeth was observing Anita in a small, language-heterogeneous work group, it was Anita who spontaneously took responsibility for introducing Elizabeth to all the children. As Judi pointed out, Anita's efforts to talk with children (and classroom visitors like Elizabeth and Anne) not dominant in Spanish supported the development of her English as well as the development of the classroom community itself.

In her presentation of Anita's work samples, Judi played audio-tapes to demonstrate Anita's code switching (her "real understanding that she is dealing in two different languages"), including her spontaneous translations from one language to the next in an effort to be clear. The tapes demonstrated as well Anita's oral facility with Spanish and English poems and songs: "When I think of poems, songs, and dances," said Judi, "I just think of her."

Judi brought samples of Anita's writing to illustrate the careful linear arrangements of letters that accompanied her small pictures of people, animals, stars, and trees. Anita's "magic writing," like most of Judi's children's, began with a mix of numbers and letters, but gradually became just letters.

Although Anita was not yet clearly making sound/symbol connections when she wrote, she did understand that oral stories could be written down in different languages. To demonstrate this, Judi focused our attention on the oral language that surrounded Anita's drawing and writing. For example, when Anita dictated "translations" of her magic writing for Judi, her Spanish-language dictations were more coherent than those in which she used English. But her use of English demonstrated her alertness to curricular content, since she made use of English language words from study units and shared songs and poems, as Judi explained:

Louise: It's her choice of language—which language she's going to tell you the story in. But which language do you usually ask her in?

Judi: Spanish. Because I really believe in maintaining the first language as the second language develops, and to have her emergent literacy skills be in her first language.

Louise: She tells a much more comprehensible story in Spanish.

Judi: Oh absolutely . . . but she has the concept of a lot of words in both languages . . . if she's heard things in English that we talk about [in our thematic units].

As an illustration of Anita's (and Judi's) sensitivity to curricular content, readers may recall Judi's earlier presented description of Anita's dictation about a drawing:

Judi: (reading Anita's dictation) "Un día había un árbol de Merry Christmas." One day there was a Merry Christmas tree. "Y venían los estars." And the stars came. *Estar.* In Spanish it is *estrellita.* The *es* is very common [for Spanish-speakers learning English]. ... "Y venía una mariposa. ..." That means, there came a butterfly ... and a bear and a monkey. Now this is coming in because we've ... been separating the farm animals from the animals in the jungle. "Y ví un ratoncito." And I saw a little mouse. That could have been because the kids knew we had to have an exterminator come in. ... "Y todas las butterflies." So you see the code switching here, instead of *mariposa*, like she said [earlier].

In a single piece, Anita had textual allusions to many key classroom themes.

Judi viewed Anita as "a kid who is just so ready to learn. She is always right there. ..." Judi was frustrated that the formal assessment tools used in her school did not reveal Anita's wealth of social and language skills, nor her intense involvement with literacy. The "Kindergarten Assessment" and the report cards emphasized a narrow band of skills, especially knowledge of letters and letter sounds. Judi taught those skills through her many literacy activities. But such a narrow perspective on a small child's "competence" greatly underestimated that child's resources and possibilities. And so it was with Anita. "I don't think [such tools] really assess where she is. ... I just feel like she's on the bridge [entering into literacy]. I have this vision of her being on this bridge and getting ready to jump over to the other side."

CAROLYN'S DARIAN: NEGOTIATING HOME, THE "Y," AND THE SCHOOL

Carolyn's School and Classroom

Carolyn's school, on a main business thoroughfare, is surrounded by spreading commercial businesses amidst apartment buildings, residential homes, and motels. It is a small school, built for 180 children, but it serves over twice that number. As testament to the school's bursting walls, there are ten portable classrooms on what was originally a playground. Although the walkway to the front of the school is lined with inviting green grass, Carolyn's school, like Judi's, has no grassy playfield for the children; it has a small asphalt playground with a climbing structure partially bound in yellow tape (inaccessible to the kids because of a lack of adequate padding). Still, Carolyn's children "lived and breathed for Wednesday . . . Structure Day," the one day of the week when her class had its turn to play on the unbound part of the structure.

Carolyn's school serves primarily African American children. In her first-grade classroom Carolyn had twenty-seven children, twenty-two of whom were African American (including Darian), two were African immigrants, two of European heritage, and one of Asian (Indian) heritage. Carolyn's school differs from Judi's, in part, because the population is ethnically and linguistically less diverse. It also differs, however, because it does not have the sort of historical relationship to parents that Judi's school has, and this issue of home/school relationship figured prominently in Carolyn's contributions to our group. Carolyn was "a real advocate for kids, and I wouldn't feel if I had a good program if I didn't meet with parents."

Carolyn had previously taught in an Oakland school in which she felt closer ties to parents, as well as colleagues. The very physical structure of her old school seemed to promote easier, more relaxed communication. That school had also had fewer children from economically strained homes than did her present school. Carolyn remembered the financial support teachers had received from the relatively affluent parent association, and the "project" support from school-savvy mothers, who have traditionally been responsible for children's "home work." Such support could be overwhelming, more a matter of "parents telling you how to do it" than collaborating with you, as some of us said. Still, in Carolyn's experience, as in that of other teachers, when the school had limited occasions for parent/teacher communication, when both families and schools were severely stressed, it was more difficult to bring children's home and school worlds together in positive ways (Lightfoot, 1978; Martin, 1992).

My school, she said, "is more of an individual classroom with your own door. . . . [At my old school] there was more of an open feeling . . . because parents and kids from other classes and staff just sort of came through your hallway and came into your room. . . . We had lots of parent volunteers when I was there. The parent group in itself was very active. They raised lots of money and teachers got individual stipends . . . to purchase materials. . . . It was more of a population of nonworking mothers at that school. . . . You had people that were from the upper-middle class and then you also had children that were on AFDC. . . . [My current school doesn't have] parent participation or volunteers to any degree. . . . It could be attributed to the fact that it [has] more of a working population . . . or because of the high AFDC [half of the school's families], who . . . are not well read in terms of what . . . to do at home with their kids [nor] the time to do it. . . . I was used to having the majority, like 75–80 percent of the kids participate in projects that we did [that required them to do part of the work at home] and [at my current school it is] really hard to get even 50 percent of the kids. . . ."

At the same time, "as much as we talk about involvement of parents there is no built-in component for me to converse or have a meeting with a parent. It is very, very frustrating because I know how important it is to include parents in what kids are doing on a day-to-day basis."

Carolyn felt she had to fight the system to realize her goal of allowing parents a part in their child's school experience. For example, she sometimes held parent teacher conferences off the school site "because I get kicked out at four; our custodian leaves and the building has to be locked up." For parents' night, "[I] sent my own invitations . . . the first week of school; I let [my parents] know and said 'Mark your calendars.' I had a plan. [The principal] said 'Oh you had a packed house [thirty or forty people]. That was great.'. . . Other people had just two and three people that night."

The value Carolyn placed on bringing children's home experiences—and their parents—into the classroom world were reflected in her talk about her own curriculum. Like others, she had an open-ended writing period; in fact, she had used Judi's term "magic writing" to encourage her children to be playful during writing time and to explore possible spellings. She also, however, talked a great deal about projects that might link school and home experiences. Readers may recall, for example, her Halloween interview project or, perhaps, the taped poems Amy and Kathy brought to school.

Carolyn's desires for bringing children's out-of-school lives into the school and for establishing good communication between parents and teachers were also evident in her portrait of "studious" but not altogether "serious" Darian, as was her sensitivity to the socioeconomic strains with which many young families struggle.

Darian's Portrait

"Today I brought Darian's work," said Carolyn one early spring evening, and she passed around a stapled set of photocopied papers. Darian, she explained, tended to throw himself into class activities and "to work with a real intensity." And this, felt Carolyn, was a real strength. At the same time, this intensity, and her classroom projects, could work together in ways that created tension at home.

"His mom is a single parent," Carolyn explained, "and she's rather young. She doesn't have a lot of opportunity—because she's a single parent working—to come in the classroom. But the few times that I've met her, she's a really warm person, and she really cares about him and wants him to learn. She feels, I think, a little guilty about not being able to put a lot of time in with him. But . . . he's really turning out to be this really great learner. . . .

"There are lots of activities that I do that I assign for homework that you have to have certain materials or tools, or you need a parent's assistance. . . . He'll tell me, 'Mom says that the homework is too hard, because I should be able to do it by myself.' My interpretation of that is that when it requires adult assistance, or requires materials that may not be right at hand, . . . she doesn't have that kind of time. . . ."

Darian spent his afterschool hours at a day care program at the school run by the YMCA; that program was his "second home," as Carolyn said. Still, that second home had no specific time for work on school projects. Those projects went home with Darian in the evening.

For example, Carolyn and her students "had an activity earlier in the year where we had a story called 'Mr. Robot,' and I had the kids use recycleable things [at home] to build their own robots, and they wrote stories about them. . . . I remember when we shared the robots on the rug, and he didn't have one, he said, 'I don't have one, and my mom wouldn't help me.' He was really disgusted with his mom. There was a lot of anger, even to the point where I remember him crying on that day. . . . [So then] I was calling his mom regarding something else, and she said, 'I'm really sorry that we weren't able to do the robot. You know, he's still mad at me about that.' And that's the kind of student he is. He really wants to be included in whatever we're doing in class; he wants to be a part."

Carolyn felt that Darian *was* an active member of the classroom community, often volunteering to share his work with the class. That volunteering was especially pleasing because Darian had trouble articulating some of his sounds and could be difficult to understand. Darian had "thrown himself" into writing as well and made remarkable progress. The journal entries Carolyn brought contained examples of Darian's early fall writing: pages filled with words copied from books and classroom charts. They also contained examples of his frequent use of familiar sentence patterns (e.g., "I like the YMCA.").

By the winter months, however, Darian showed a playfulness in his use of selected words. A favorite of Carolyn's was his drawing of a dinosaur, lying prone, tongue hanging out. "The dinosaur is dead. Oh no!" reads the brief text. And, by spring, Darian was one of Carolyn's children who seemed to find a written, conversational voice. His journal contained entries about his good and bad days on the playground, at home, and most especially, at the YMCA. Below is the entry Darian had written about playing football at the "Y":

> Fet Ball is my Teg I liKe FeT Ball I Live Pallyg cah ho yes I like Fet Ball et is my Teg ho Yes I can tor good Be cez I pall ehve Day. By Darian
>
> [Football is my thing. I like football. I love playing catch. Oh yes. I like football. It is my thing. Oh yes. I can throw good because I play everyday. By Darian]

These entries, composed with invented spellings and often accompanied by detailed pictures, reflected, Carolyn thought, Darian's increasing confidence in himself as a writer and, also, his sense of what he could accomplish through writing. In fact, writing was a major way in which Carolyn found out about Darian's relationships in and out of school. Darian was "the sort of kid you could go the whole day and not necessarily connect with him because he will just go about his business. . . ." Observing and talking with him as he wrote, listening to him read from his journal, and responding to the letters he sent through the class mailbox were major avenues of connection with Darian, who was quite forthcoming about his feelings:

> I do nit like wa pepo do nit paly wes me I Fel PuT Downs.
>
> [I do not like when people do not play with me. I feel put down.]

Indeed, when Elizabeth observed in Carolyn's room, she listened to Carolyn and Darian have a few minutes chat about his writing, and, in the process, she learned that Darian had no siblings, that he sometimes visited his Grandma, that he loved to go to his "tete's" because "she got six kids at her house," that actually "she got five," but when he goes over there "she got six," and so he had lots of people to play with over there!

Carolyn had brought examples of Darian's responses to more structured writing activities, in which the children reimagined or reworked material from stories they had read together. For one such text, Carolyn's children had retold a story from their literature reader called "Boo Bear Takes a Rest" (McPhail, 1989). These stories feature a sweet boy bear and his family and friends, but the children's Boo Bear stories "got to be really gory; they were kind of violent" and "not at all like the McPhail stories." Quiet, studious Darian's featured the decidedly horrific film character Freddie Kruger: "Boo Bear went to sleep. And he has nightmares about Freddie Kruger. Freddie Kruger has a fight with Boo Bear."

Another of Darian's texts was based on a shared children's book, *Millions of Cats* ([Gag, 1977], a book with what many in our group viewed as a horrific ending—cats devouring cats). Carolyn had used this activity to provide a familiar language play (i.e., the book's repetitive refrain) as support for children's own language play. Darian's read:

> <u>Dogs</u> here,
>
> <u>Dogs</u> there,
>
> <u>Dogs</u> and
>
> <u>Puppies</u> everywhere,
>
> Hundreds of <u>Dogs</u>
>
> Thousands of <u>Dogs</u>
>
> Millions and billions and trillions of <u>Dogs</u>.

(Darian filled blank lines in the verse with the underlined words; but he also added a line all his own):

> <u>Infinity of Dogs here and there</u>.

This activity seemed to serve as a kind of "aha moment" for Darian. As Carolyn explained, "You [Kristin] were mentioning that [Darian's writing samples suggested that, in March] he just started to grow. I remember this as one of those 'aha!' moments for him. After he wrote it, he went around, and he was sticking it in everyone's face. He was saying, 'Can I read my poem to you? <u>Dogs</u> here, <u>Dogs</u> there, and then I put this part in. Mrs. McBride didn't tell me to, but I put it in. <u>Infinity of Dogs here and there</u>.' He must have read it to six kids. I stood back and watched him and realized that the confidence had oozed over. . . . And then he stayed after school because he wanted to read it to me again. So I made him a copy of that because it was like one of his favorite things that he had done on his own. . . . [All of the children] really liked the *Millions of Cats* story . . . but I thought that *Millions of Cats* was kind of gruesome myself."

At this point, Carolyn's ambivalence about the "gory" Boo Bear stories and the "gruesome" *Millions of Cats* led our group into an extended discussion of the value of children's critical and creative rewriting of stories from the school library and the popular media (see Chapter 4). We wanted the children to feel as if they all had "the license and freedom," as Carolyn said, to reconsider words and worlds. And we understood that fostering such freedom required ongoing and deliberate action by a teacher willing to engage with the less appealing aspects of children's worlds; teaching was, to use Kristin's words, a matter of "trying to free" children's imaginations.

On the other hand, Carolyn's pleasure in the image of Darian running around her room, "sticking it in people's faces," was another example of children's pleasure in making their individual contribution to the classroom community, and the potential for writing to be one means to that end. Indeed, it was the importance for Darian of public sharing, of being part of the community, that made Carolyn particularly distressed when, near the end of the year, Darian began to complain about certain children teasing him about his speech.

Carolyn brought this teasing to the attention of our group the evening in which Louise talked about Penny, a severely physically disabled child. Louise discussed her efforts to integrate Penny into the social life of her class, efforts that involved, in part, assuring the other children that Penny's disabilities could not be "caught" and, also, that those disabilities did not prevent her from participating in classroom projects.

"I would imagine," Carolyn said in response, "that [the children have] a lot of questions." And then she told us about Darian.

Carolyn: Just within the last two to three weeks, he's now being teased and mimicked because of the way he speaks. It's amazing to me that he has been speaking this way since day one and they've just come to the awareness of it. So today with a group of kids who were doing the teasing, he came in and complained to me. I sat down with them, and we talked about it. . . . I told them that I was disappointed because they were teasing him. . . .

Anne: I guess the big implication is that we have to talk about what the kids notice, and that they're talking and thinking about lots of things that are uncomfortable.

Carolyn: It's hard. . . . You don't know what to say, or how much you should say, or how uncomfortable you are making this [child with the perceived difference] in sharing. So I really tried to handle it today where I told some, and then would turn to Darian and say, "Do you want to tell them about when you go to speech, and who you go with, and what you do there?" He said, "Sure" and started to tell them. . . .

Darian's comfort with himself and Carolyn's class helped her handle the situation.

Indeed, Carolyn's own report, and her need to get samples of Darian's talk and writing, seemed in and of itself to be a source of great pleasure to him, the pleasure of having one's efforts acknowledged:

Carolyn: [I] told him that I was coming [here] . . . and sharing, and he said, "Who are these teachers?" I said, "They're people from different schools." And he said, "Are you going to take everybody's stuff?" And I said, "No, I'm just going to take yours. . . ." So he said, "Well, you should tell them that at first I didn't get it, and then one day I went home, and then I got it. So that's why I can write this now." And I said, "I'll make sure that I tell them that's what happened." So he wanted you to know that he didn't always know this.

He wanted us to know that he had figured out this writing business, and so we did.

JILL'S KATHERINE: FINDING A PLACE IN THE CULTURE OF THE FAMILY AND THE SCHOOL

Jill's School and Classroom

Unlike Judi's and Carolyn's schools, the buildings and portables that comprise Jill's school are clustered on a tree-shaded lot. The school serves a relatively small number of students—about 250 children from diverse ethnic backgrounds. During the project year, over half the children were African American, and the others were of varied backgrounds. In Jill's own second grade, the twenty-eight children included fifteen African American children, three European American children, and the rest were of varied Asian, Latino, Middle Eastern, and biracial heritages.

The school's small size would seem to lend itself to a close-knit faculty, a school community. But Jill, who had taught at the school for ten years, had felt her sense of community ebbing away. Over the years, trusted colleagues left, and the remaining faculty had little say in the hiring of new colleagues; thus, Jill felt, the shared values and philosophies that had held the faculty together were becoming diffuse. And this mattered to Jill, because colleagues had been key to her own sense of professional growth. In her words, "I've always had someone there to support me."

In addition to collegiality and community, Jill stressed the importance of diversity to her professional life. Her appreciation of diversity was rooted, she said, in her childhood, when her father introduced her to the African American culture thriving in St. Paul, Minnesota. That appreciation was furthered during her many years as a teacher of deaf students, from infancy through secondary school, in programs for the children of migrant workers, for those labeled "emotionally disturbed" or simply "special education."

"It doesn't matter," said Jill, "whether you can hear or you can't hear, you can see or you can't see, whether you speak Spanish or German or you sign—whatever it is, I see that we all have that need for a community. We all have that need to have a voice of some sort, . . . and I think that our need for language shapes most of our lives. . . .

"I'm listening around the table, and we have so many minicultures, and we're trying to find that balance of the minicultures within a culture where we are all accepting of the differences and realizing that we are all different but we're more alike than we are different."

Jill's emphasis on a community of the whole was evident in her discussions of her literacy curriculum, as was her valuing of diverse human experiences. Her students wrote for a range of purposes, among them, to correspond through letters, to record notes on research topics, to produce research reports to be shared, plays to be enacted; each purpose was related to an ongoing classroom project. In her narratives about her children's writing, Jill emphasized both individual decision making and group collaboration, and the ways in which both individuals and groups contributed to, and participated in, the life of the community of the whole.

Moreover, Jill stressed her students' critical awareness of how difference figured into our national history; readers may recall, for example, her students going "bonkers" over the book *Nettie's Trip South,* and their puzzlement about a story in which a woman could not take action for herself but needed her husband to act for her. Thus Jill, like others in our group, modeled a linkage often recommended by those concerned with multicultural education: a link between critical literacy and appreciation of different human experiences (Sleeter & Grant, 1987; Perry & Fraser, 1993).

Jill's concerns about community and her "embrace" of differences were evident in her portrait of Katherine, a second grader who, de- spite her reputation as a problematic student, made solid literacy progress. In Jill's portrait, that progress was linked, on the one hand, to the ways in which literacy activities helped Katherine find a place in the classroom community and, on the other hand, to the ways in which those activities contributed to Katherine's place in the cultural life of her family.

Katherine's Portrait

Near the end of our project meetings, Jill introduced us to Katherine, a child who, by her own self-report, had been waiting quite a while for someone to teach her to read and write. Katherine was Tongan and "proud of her heritage," said Jill. Katherine had a "loving relationship with her brothers and sisters, and in fact, they come and get her after school every day. They share their days with one another." Still, as the second girl in a family of four children, she felt "kind of on the bottom."

"What has happened in the family . . . is that the oldest girl reaps all of the attention and has all of the responsibilities of the family as far as carrying·on the traditions. . . . And of course then Robert [her brother] gets attention because he's the oldest boy. And then the youngest girl gets a lot of attention. . . . Katherine's kind of left in the middle. . . . And the mother has explained to me that that truly is what's happening in the family."

In the first grade, Katherine was also "kind of on the bottom." Here the problem was not getting attention but her reported inability to pay attention. Katherine "started at our school last year in first grade. Her first-grade teacher shared with me, saying 'Katherine's very inattentive. . . . She can't sit still and she's all over the place. . . . She can't focus on any specific activity for longer than five minutes. She can't read, she can't write.' So I got this long list of 'she can'ts.' I said, 'Can you give me some of her strengths?' 'Well, she's sweet.' 'Give me more.' 'She's very loving. And she likes to draw.' So she felt like those were her only strengths."

Despite her negative advance billing, Katherine seemed "very excited" to be in Jill's second grade. But, just a couple of weeks into the school year, the classes were reconfigured (in the interest of distributing the children evenly among the classes), and Katherine was moved out. Then, six weeks later, another reconfiguration, and Katherine once again arrived in Jill's classroom, accompanied by yet another teacher report: "'She's all over the room. She can't sit down. I just wanted to let you be aware of the situation.'"

So Katherine reentered the class, and she *was* likely to move around the room; therefore, Jill helped her move: "We'd move her maybe every ten or fifteen minutes. 'Sit over here with somebody.' And then, 'OK, now you're ready to move up here.'" Jill soon learned Katherine herself had strong opinions about her reading and writing: she did not know how to and she desperately wanted to learn. Moreover, despite having been gone for six weeks, Katherine (like the other nine returning children) wanted to do the writing projects most everyone else had gotten to do, including the Frog and Toad puppet plays.

So Katherine picked a writing partner, Ebony, another "reconfigured" child and one also needing "confidence." With Jill's help, the two girls relied on their sense of oral play, as well as their knowledge of the structure and language of Frog and Toad stories, to write those two characters a new adventure:

Jill: I noticed that they would play-act with this [story]. They had a good time with it. . . . "You want to be Frog?" "You want to be Toad?" . . . It's actually one of the cutest stories. [Below is the first draft of their story.]

Frag and Tod have a paobm [problem]. Ocn [one] day Frag was in his has [house]. Tod kama [came] ranea [running] by. Tod sad to Frag caed [can] I bear [borrow] a box. NO sad Frag because I nad [need] the box. Bt [But] I am maoang [moving] sad [said] Tod. Bt I am maoang too sad Frag. War [Where] ar you maoang sad Frag. I am maoang in a peck [pink] has sad Tod. BUT I am maoang in the peck has sad Frag. hae [Hey] we or bof [both] maoang in the peck has sad Tod. You or rit [right] sad Frag. Bt wo [who] was gan [going] to uws [use] the box sad Tod. You or rit sad Frag. I now [know] sad Tod. We or bof [both] maoang in the peck has. We can bof [both] sar [share] the box. you or rit sad Tod. The ead.

As [their story] started to move along, you could hear them sitting over on the bench in front of the computer: "No, I'm moving into the pink house." "No, I'm moving into the pink house." So they'd try on the two different characters.

Anne: Did they do it orally?

Jill: They were doing it orally. I encouraged them to talk through everything. . . . "Did you like [what you just said]? Write it down. If you liked it, write it down." So they'd write it. So there is that process that they went through. They both really enjoyed writing this story. . . . And this wasn't even doing the puppet show yet; this was just writing it!

Katherine, then, wrote with the social support of her teacher and a friend, who helped her stay engaged with the task. Moreover, she wrote within the familiar context of oral play, and toward the desired end goal of a puppet play about two well-known literary characters. And, to add to the pleasure, Katherine had access to a technological tool that she was most anxious to use—the computer (a desire Katherine's mother had told Jill about).

By providing all this support, and good fun, Jill allowed Katherine to figure out that, in fact, "she already knew how to write. So it was acknowledging her skills that she already had that really helped her to start gaining some confidence and self-esteem. . . ." This self-confidence went home, in the form of a polished, computer-produced final draft, which Katherine "thrust into the hands" of her family, especially her older sister and brother.

In addition to the Frog and Toad story, Jill also brought examples of Katherine's writing that were related to a class study of animals interconnected with the baobab tree. Katherine had a research piece on one member of that animal community, the jaguar (which she had drawn expertly), and a folktale about another member, the "elegant grasshopper." Both of these written products, like the puppet show activity, engaged Katherine in the social life of the classroom and, in addition, allowed her to use her oral and artistic skills.

For example, Jill explained the complex skills Katherine drew on—and the complex decisions she made—in writing a folktale about the "elegant grasshopper," a folktale like those told by the human community interconnected with the baobab tree. Among Katherine's decisions were: the topic, the story characters and plot, the physical features of her drawn "elegant grasshopper," the arrangement of text and picture on a page, the formatting of the text itself, and the kind of punctuation marks needed. Since Katherine's eyes "jump around the page, and she has a very difficult time reading," she decided to spread her story out, using the dialogue format she and Ebony had learned from the Frog and Toad books. One draft of Katherine's story follows:

> One day Grasshopper was in his house. His fridne Elephant came over.
>
> "Hellow" said Elephant.

"Hellow" said Grasshopper.

"Elephant I want to learn to hop" said Grasshopper.

"Ok" said Elephant. "but you have to help me find my babie" said Elephant. . . .

They went to the park. Graspper stood on a rock and jumped.

I jumped said Grasshoppe. . .

Good said Elephant but now you have to help me find my babie. . .

Jill did not present Katherine as someone free of difficulties with the conventions of writing and reading. But she did present Katherine as a young child growing both in her sense of her own options as a literate person, and in her confidence as a decision maker, who considered what, with whom, and how to write. At the same time, Jill emphasized how Katherine's literate skills supported her growing sense of herself as a learner. Katherine, Jill said, especially loved the idea that animals have responsibilities to families and communities, and shared ways of doing things or "cultures," just like humans do, just like Katherine herself did.

"It's exciting. She's starting to see everything kind of connect for her. . . . It's great for her, coming in, and people saying she couldn't write, she couldn't read, she couldn't spell, and then seeing that this child really was capable and could do all of that. . . .

"She [told me], 'You know, I really love to write, and I write at home a lot, and I make up stories a lot.' And the wonderful thing that she shared with me, and her mother actually shared with me [too], she said, 'after the lights go out at night, I crawl in Ani's bed' (who is her older sister). 'And we get the flashlight and read and read and read. Sometimes it's real late. That's why sometimes . . . I'm really tired. . . .' So when her mom shared with me, she said, 'I'm really torn.' And I said, 'I can understand that because it's such a wonderful thing for her to do with her older sister. . . . I would hate to take that away from her or Ani.'" Indeed, when Anne was visiting in Jill's room, Katherine told her that she liked writing "better than recess!"

Jill's positive presentation of Katherine was undergirded by a broad definition of literacy, one involving many means of communicating, and reflecting on, experience. And yet, like everyone in the group, Jill knew Katherine would look much less competent if that definition were confined to a score on an achievement test. She did not want Katherine, or any of her children, to be reduced from learners to test scores.

Jill: We have just finished the CTBS [California Test of Basic Skills], and in the second grade there are a lot of biased questions. We talked about them. In fact, we got to one where it presupposed or assumed they had experiences with parades. . . . Most of them had never seen a parade. . . . We got to this part, and they were looking and saying, "Parade?" And they looked at me, and they said, "Is this one of those biased ones?" And I said, "Yes, you're going to be able to pick them out, when you start to see that if you haven't had the experience, it's very hard to relate to the question."

But the worst part they were talking about today . . . the spelling part, which was very unfair. . . . One guy said, "Who makes up these questions?" And I said, "That's a good question. Various people are hired by the company that prints it, that makes money off of selling these tests to the districts like us." . . . I don't teach spelling formally. They learn it in their writing, and they learn rules. But they had every irregular spelling you could think of. . . .

Louise: And do you have to choose the one that's right or the one that's wrong?

Jill: They have to choose the one that's right out of four very close spellings, like "once": *once, onse, wnce, wonse.*

Louise: A very visual memory.

Carolyn: Which doesn't match at all with what we do with invented spelling [i.e., with our emphasis on having children take good guesses based, in part, on their knowledge of how words sound].

Judi: That's right.

Jill: It's awful. So I said, "Just do the best you can."

Kristin: . . . And even the comprehension part. . . . Just the other day, [we] were listing ways to [compose] beginnings and end[ings of stories]. . . . And [the children] had this huge list. . . . And then they get to [the exam], and . . . [it's one] right answer.

Jill: I know. My kids said it was pretty awful. And I said, "If we learn anything from it, we'll learn test-taking techniques" [i.e., the process of eliminating answers, of doing the easiest ones first, of looking at the beginning sounds of words and using context]. Because I taught them test-taking techniques. It was helpful to Katherine.

Carolyn: But I've found for first graders, almost everything they read is large print, and we use a lot of "Big Books," then they get to the test, and it's in microprint. And then the format, it's very adult-like for them, so it's very intimidating. . . . And then using words that they really don't know. . . . The names are just awful. Even just using Tom, Dick, Sally, and Jane would be better than some of the names that they had. . . .

Kristin: We had, I think, Milly and Rhoda.

Carol: In the third grade, they try to be ethnic. So they have these *names.*

Jill: It's hard. Katherine said, "Why don't they have words we can spell?"

Jill, like all of us, was more interested in what Katherine could do than what she couldn't do. Moreover, Jill's comments on testing, at the end of this case presentation, opened up yet another discussion, one about the assumptions test writers make about children's lives—and teacher's lives too. Jill talked about helping children gain a critical perspective on the texts in their lives, including those tests; she aimed to help them understand that those texts were written by somebody for some reason in some time and place. She and her children would do "their test," but, Jill hoped, they would resist giving the test makers power over their vision of themselves.

Thus Jill closed her portrait of Katherine as she had begun it, with a concern that Katherine not be limited—whether by her past "record" or her current "achievement scores." Rather, Jill wanted us to picture a child who was growing "in leaps and bounds" beyond that record and those scores. And we did.

Summary: "What Did You Think of Me?"

These portraits of Anita, Darian, and Katherine are three of the eighteen formally presented—and of the many more brief images of children who emerged in our talk. Each of these three narratives was shaped by a teacher, with her own life history and professional place, with her own characteristic thematic emphases. And each had chosen a child from a different sort of familial situation, a situation structured by the interplay of economic circumstance and cultural tradition—a family that crossed national borders, one that extended beyond the nuclear unit to include cousins (and a second home at the "Y"), and one of close siblings with expected family roles. But, despite these differences, each portrait contributed—as all did—to a vision of teaching and learning as nested in the complexities of institutional structures, negotiated human relations, and instructional activities.

The emerging child portraits of Anita, Darian, and Katherine were intertwined with the possibilities and constraints of their respective schools. Those institutions assigned (and reassigned) them their slots in the system, as speakers of certain languages, as people of certain ages, as students with certain "reputations" from day cares and past grades. But institutional indices of grade, language, and reported past performance did not define these children, nor did their cultural category or socioeconomic circumstance. Indeed, it was in the interplay of institutional structure and sociocultural circumstance that "differences" from the assumed norm most often emerged as "problems," the "problems," for example, of children speaking varied languages, having an employed single parent, and not entering school with institutionally expected expertise in print conventions.

In the teachers' detailed narratives, each child was a complex, changing person, deeply involved in learning; and the vision of each child's sociocultural experiences and language resources was shaped by the human and material possibilities of the classroom itself. As members of the classroom community, the children potentially had the social support of work partners and appreciative audiences, the interactional support of familiar languages and oral genres (e.g., storytelling to a trusted adult, collaborative play with a friend), and the content support of interesting topics to talk, read, and write about.

Moreover, in classroom activities, children's engagement with print was couched within projects that involved not only their writing and reading but also their drawing, talking, acting, consulting, organizing, and on and on. There were many ways to enter into school literacy and, once engaged, the community resources, detailed above, could potentially involve children in increasingly more complex decision making about, and constructing with, print itself. Further, those in-school activities could potentially make space for children's talk, writing, and reading about their out-of-school experiences with families, friends, and the imagined figures of popular media. These child texts, like those offered by adult authors, were potential sources of critical imagination, of wondering about how stories (and lives) could be told differently.

Thus, these experienced teachers, like all of us, told stories of high expectations, of children growing, even as these very stories led us to articulate serious concerns—about the provision for native language support for all children, about links between home and school, about collegial relations and institutionalized tests. Most of us were involved in one way or another with professional reform outside the classroom (e.g., working on new report card forms, on mentor programs for new teachers, on science and mathematics curricula). But, in the end, what mattered most was how these efforts influenced, and were influenced by, life on the inside. Consider, for example, one last conversational excerpt, which begins with a reference to out-of-classroom efforts for school assessment reform and gradually becomes interwoven with references to our own efforts and our own reflections on classroom life:

Carol: I think when assessment changes, teaching will change. . . .

Linda: Sometimes I think if we get in there and change the report card, other things will come along with it. We will be able to focus on literacy development, instead of individual letters. . . .

Judi: It goes back to what we were talking about before, what do we consider as real literacy development?

Carolyn: When we're talking about literacy, is it just the ABC's or can we have a new definition?

Linda: Or I was thinking about Jill, and her dialogue with her students, the idea of students having a voice in the classroom. That needs to be in there.

Jill: And putting people in roles, giving them a real part in the classroom and their learning.

Carolyn: And they're empowered by that . . .

and so, of course, are teachers involved in a project that gives them a real part in ongoing professional learning. As individuals, we sometimes straggled into our Tuesday meetings exhausted . . . but left buoyed by intellectual reflection, collegial support and, of course, our mutual pleasure in knowing the young.

Chapter **6** | Extending the Conversation

"It's Not about Telling You What to Do"

> Power is the ability to take one's place in whatever discourse is essential to action and the right to have one's part matter.
>
> **C. G. Heilbrun,** *Writing a Woman's Life*

This book is not, in Jill's words, about "telling [teachers] what to do." Rather, it is about classroom teachers' experiences with children's differences and about how those experiences are realized within the contexts of schools as institutional structures, as webs of human relations, and as hubs of enacted activities.

In presenting these experiences, we have aimed to inspire others' reflections. This goal is undergirded by a passionate belief that there are no simplistic prescriptions, no ten easy steps for teaching in and for a nation "of many voices" (Smitherman, 1990, p. 111). Rather, such teaching requires a willingness to be "lifelong learners," as Carolyn said, especially since children, communities, curricular contexts, and institutional structures constantly change.

Such learners—always busy, often exhausted—do want to "stay abreast of reform and changes . . . of [university] research," to continue with Carolyn's words. But, as everyone said, they need time, and, moreover, they need to feel like their intelligence, their voices, their experiences as the prime adult school actors matter. This means not only that they learn from each other and from administrators, consultants, and university researchers and educators (as one-time public school teacher

Anne has become), but also that outside experts learn from the inside ones (as Anne has done).

In Celia Genishi's words (1992, p. 204), "people do not see themselves as *actors,* people who accomplish things, unless someone demonstrates that they are actors, unless someone places them in a story." In this chapter educators based outside the classroom and, moreover, at a distance from our group, help us illustrate the potential power of shared experiences by bringing our talk into their conversations about diversity and teaching. In the sections ahead, Celia Genishi and Jerrie Cobb Scott, both educators and researchers who now work at universities, and Alice Kawazoe, the educator and administrator who helped launch our group, complete our collective speaking turn by beginning their own (an editorial strategy inspired by Mikhail Bakhtin, literary theorist and philosopher about difference [1986]).

Celia Genishi begins with the complexities of negotiating cultural identity in a university classroom on the other end of the country from us, in New York City. She then intertwines our voices with those of the classroom teachers she knows as educator and researcher, and, in so doing, she highlights one important thread of our dialogue—that of dealing with the "audible difference" of linguistic diversity.

On the Yin-Yang of Teaching:
When Does Difference Make a Difference?
Celia Genishi
Teachers College, Columbia University

What difference does difference make? The question calls to mind the yin-yang of teaching—not in terms of an opposition between feminine (yin) and masculine (yang), but in terms of the need to hold in mind opposing ideas in order to form a whole. My answer to this difficult question is paradoxical: difference makes "all the difference" at times and "not much difference at all" at other times. The question also provokes a rush of images, images of children's faces, adults' faces, classrooms with young children and with adults as students. The adults are often teachers participating in my classes or workshops at Teachers College, located in New York City, where the differences of race, ethnicity, economics, language, religion, politics, and so on are evident and palpable. It is a place where differences are taken for granted in many ways, and where differences are celebrated and inequities are worried over intensely.

Teachers of course celebrate and worry over the difference that difference makes in their classrooms. Their worries are, I think, captured concisely in the questions of the titles of Chapters 2 and 3: "Who am I to them?" and "What are you?" These questions have been in the air around discussions I have with classroom teachers, prospective teachers, administrators, and teacher educators. Particularly in a class in which students and I focus on social factors related to classroom practices, issues of difference are focal.

What impresses me about the East Bay teachers' discussions and descriptions of their elementary classrooms is not only that the teachers remind me of those teachers I know and work with, but that their children remind me of both the teachers and myself as we all try to sort out how social factors of difference, such as race and gender, influence learning and teaching. In one class the students (most of whom are teachers) and I reflect the kind of diversity the East Bay teachers describe in theirs—we are mostly North American by birth, and also African American, European American, Haitian, Japanese, Korean, Puerto Rican, and combinations of these. We tell anecdotes about how social factors enter into our daily lives to begin to build a sense of community—to begin to see and define for ourselves "what we are" and "who we are."

We also try to see "who we are to them" and "who we could be to them." After hearing how Andrea Smith, who had been the only African American student in her school in a Northeastern suburb, had often been cruelly insulted and harassed, Lisa Martone, a teacher of European American descent, said, "I hope you don't mind my asking, but what would you have wanted your teachers to do for you?" Or, who would you have wanted your teachers to be for you?

The response from Andrea was that she remembered and appreciated one teacher who made her feel special, by things that she said, her body language, and other small but noticeable behaviors. That ability to make each student feel "special" suggests again a yin-yang response. The teacher may have based her approach on contrasting principles: both to be blind to differences ("*all* students deserve the same treatment") and to be sensitive to them ("each student at some time needs special attention because of his or her *individual differentness*"). These individual differences, such as racial difference and the behaviors it prompts from peers, are noticed amidst all that teachers do, think about, feel, let pass, or notice in the array of voices and actions that make up classroom activity.

An Audible Difference: Linguistic Diversity in the Classroom

The classrooms of a number of the East Bay teachers illustrated a difference that is becoming increasingly noticeable in North American classrooms. That difference is "voice"; one hears the voices of many learners whose first language is not English. Since this is a difference (a *horizontal* one in the East Bay teachers' terms) that has a clear and major effect on the learners' ability to participate in classroom activity, teachers everywhere generally make adjustments for the English as a Second Language (ESL) learner, ranging from speaking more slowly to changing the nature of learners' work.

Cira Focarino, a first-grade teacher in a New York City public school with a large Cantonese-speaking population, made these kinds of adjustments (for *vertical* differences among learners) as she and her students created dialogue journals. Yet Cira also articulated a paradox—that less knowledge of English both does and does not make a difference. She said, "Language is language as long as they [the children] are using it," but goes on to qualify the statement:

> I make them blend, and I don't really look at them as my ESL. Everyone needs the same kinds of skills more or less. They [the ESL students] may need more labeling, you know, have a sense of the names of these things that everybody is

talking about in English. They may know them in Chinese; they may not. (Genishi, Dubetz, & Focarino, in press)

Thus Cira needs to provide the "names of these things" to some children and not others. When revising what children have written in their journals, she suggests to one child whose English is just budding to change one word in his entry, whereas she asks a comfortably bilingual child to edit for clarity and preciseness. Cira is not oblivious to vertical differences in linguistic ability and so does not treat each child "equally" with respect to the details of instruction. Ultimately, though, she views every child as a language learner with the potential to become an English speaker/reader/writer; in that respect they are not different from each other.

In her efforts to create a flexible language-based curriculum, Cira was supported by a principal and colleagues whose views about language learning were compatible with hers. Like Judy in Oakland, she also worked in a neighborhood where there was one dominant language other than English. There are of course many teachers in other circumstances, where district or school mandates conflict with teacher politics, preference, or knowledge or where, as in Elise's and Judi's Oakland classrooms, multiple languages are spoken.

In one such classroom in New York, a kindergarten teacher worked to bring a roomful of ESL learners—from seven different language groups—into an English-speaking school culture (Fassler, 1995). The teacher, Ms. Barker, had been trained to teach ESL and managed, as the sole English speaker in the classroom, to give all her children opportunities to begin the process of becoming English users. She established a simple but powerful tacit rule, "Talk whenever possible," and through talk—either in English or a child's home language—the classroom became a place where children also learned the fundamentals of literacy and math, as well as the fundamentals of how to be a social participant in this place called school.

In Ms. Barker's school, ESL children were all grouped in a single class—a less than ideal situation for learning English; English-speaking peer "models" could certainly have enhanced opportunities to learn more. (Further this was not a situation to encourage maintenance of children's home languages as Ms. Barker knew only English.) This teacher resembles the East Bay teachers who feel strong institutional constraints, yet work within them so that despite difficult circumstances children learn.

In a roomful of "different" children, Ms. Barker treated them in some ways with utmost equality. For example, she never turned away a child who had a question or was waiting for her attention, and she was never heard to forbid the use of home language. She also clarified and repeated words and concepts in a way that suggested that every child was entitled to her "input." Yet if some children persisted in relying on their home language, she did not force the use of English. Although learning English was a principal aim in Ms. Barker's room, she consistently balanced equality with recognition of difference.

Making a Difference while Respecting Complexity

Linguistic difference is an especially evident one that teachers must take into account at the same time that they attend to other key differences of culture. The East Bay teachers evidence broad knowledge of a variety of cultures, including their own. They also have specific information regarding the history and customs of diverse groups. As they acknowledge and highlight this information, they and their children work to name and understand the complexity of differences. For example, Carolyn cited an example in which a child who is part African American was told by another child that he was *not* Black, whereas a child who identifies herself as white was told she was not white, only "fair-skinned." Stating "what we are" was far more complex than many adults would predict, as the subtleties of race and nationality appeared to be *negotiated* and not taken for granted.

At the same time, when seeking examples of children's own understandings of cultural markers, the East Bay teachers found certain "universals" instead of typical (stereotypical?) differences. Wanda, for example, talked about how Edward, a boy of Mexican heritage, did not identify with Mexican American characters in a book whose birthday parties included pinatas and dancing. Edward said his family just went out and got a cake and came home, suggesting that they were no different from most folks. Similarly, Kesha, a child in Linda's kindergarten, initiated a "Sizzler ritual," in which a restaurant routine was enacted at will during free-choice time. Thus the children's symbols of status and inclusion did not fit into predictable "ethnic" categories. Both children and teachers seemed to resist easy naming or categorization.

The valuing of difference, then, is a process that is as varied and complex as the human being working to figure out and respect differences. What that process should look like—whether it should look one way for certain children and another way for others—is not at all clear. What is clear is that the East Bay teachers, like Adrienne Rich, have made a commitment "to ally themselves with possibilities, to make a positive difference in the changing version of America taking shape around them" (Chapter 1, p. 1, this volume).

To make that difference they live with the challenge of what I called the yin-yang of teaching. They have the capacity to hold in mind apparently opposing ideas to form a workable whole. They behave as if difference *is* critical; they see difference and uniqueness in each child and assist in making the vertical adjustments in knowledge and skill that vary across individual learners. Yet they also see that in the broadest sense difference is *not* always relevant: they expect all children to be learners who are equally deserving of respect and attention. They bravely seek that precarious and delicate balance between equality and the meaningful appreciation of difference.

While Celia Genishi emphasizes teacher-student interaction in the negotiation of difference, Jerrie Cobb Scott emphasizes interaction between classroom teachers and university researchers about difference. She begins, though, by recalling another conversation, this one between two academics, and then goes on to illustrate ways in which the unique experiences of teachers may enrich all such conversations about the difficulties of negotiating difference in schools.

Practice What You Preach; Preach What You Practice
Jerrie Cobb Scott
Central State University

In my first reading of this volume there emerged a subtext: practice what you preach. I then recalled that this subtext was similar to the one that evolved from my first in-depth conversation with Anne Haas Dyson. Boldly, Anne posed the question of how to deal with the differences between our worlds and those of the children who find their ways into our hearts through our research and academic lives. As a specific example, she related a story of her experience with trying to get a simple response to so simple a question as "What is your address?" An "I don't know" to this question seems on first blush to be a kind of stay-out-of-my-business resistance response. Boldness moved to remorse as Anne went on to explain that the child was homeless. The reality of this "true" answer set the context for a provocative conversation about the seriousness of the topic of diversity, literacy, and the urban school experience of the so-called "nonmainstream" student. An equally provocative conversation results in response to the question, "What difference does difference make?" In many ways, the book is like an extension of this first conversation, except that it has many more participants and therefore more views about how to make life in the urban classroom a more meaningful, productive experience.

During the conversation with Anne, I recall trying to focus her attention on one of the experience-based axioms that evolved from my work in urban schools and that had pushed me toward a deeper level of involvement in my own work: when faced with harsh circumstantial differences, establish a balance between what you can do and what you cannot do. Now I wanted her to practice what I was preaching, the subtext of our conversation. As the conversation continued, I realized that Anne had put in place several practices that were in keeping with Scott's axiom. Why, then, was she so appreciative of my "words of wisdom?"

In retrospect, the value of my advice had less to do with her practice than with how she thought about her practice. And for me, the conversation and its import was that somehow in that conversation Anne repackaged her way of thinking about her practices. And so, the second subtext of our conversation became: preach what you practice. Thus, in my second reading of the manuscript, "Preach What You Practice" emerged as the second subtext of this volume. My intent here is to elaborate on the two subtexts.

Practice What You Preach

This book demonstrates teaching successes in bridging the gap between theory/research and practice. Bridging that gap has been a recurring theme in discussions of research and theory on teaching and learning (including in *Classroom Environments: Multidirectional Relationships between Theory and Practice,* a book that I am co-authoring with Jacqueline Jones Royster and Delores Straker). This volume confirms our belief that many teachers are practicing what educational researchers and theorists are preaching. Contrary to popular belief, these effective practices are not simply informed by theory and research—they are also informed by what Shulman (1987) calls "the wisdom of practice." Indeed, the book makes explicit the implicit understandings that teachers have about teaching and learning, particularly in relation to differences that make a difference in how we structure learning environments.

Among the practices of the East Bay teachers that are preached by theorists and researchers are those having to do with constructivists' theories. Teachers' practices demonstrate key tenets of constructivist theory, for example, student-based meaning making and teacher-based scaffolding. Their case studies not only tell but also show us how teachers operate in the "zone of proximal development." Vygotsky defines that zone as "the distance between the actual developmental level as determined by independent problem solving and the level of potential development as determined through problem solving under adult guidance or in collaboration with more capable peers" (1978, p. 87). Also evolving out of the work is teachers' own sense making about how to operationalize "common instructional cliches," also associated with constructivism: building on what children know; creating a community of learners; educating for democracy. Thus, the subtext of Practice What They (the theorists and researchers) Preach is reflected in this work, standing as a demonstration that many "good" (effective) teachers have crossed the bridge between practice and theory, but not just on the knowledge constructed by theorists and researchers, but also on the knowledge constructed from their own "wisdom of practice."

Beyond the classrooms of the individual authors there remain, however, barriers to practicing what theorists or classroom teachers view as best practices for diverse student populations. This is revealed most directly through the distinction made between horizontal differences ("differences of language, cultural style, familial circumstance or other 'differences that shouldn't mean one person is any better than another'" [Chapter 1, p.11, this volume]) and vertical differences ("differences in where children fall on the very narrow band of abilities and skills that mark even young children as 'smart' or 'not,' 'ready' or 'not,' 'at risk' or 'not'" [Chapter 1, p.11, this volume]). A connection can be made between vertical-horizontal differences and the equity-excellence dilemma. From an institutional perspective, the vertical differences represent measures of school accountability. Equity and excellence are often linked to performance on standardized tests—how many nonmainstream students show excellence as measured by standardized tests and how far the school has come in reducing the performance gap between mainstream and nonmainstream students. From a classroom perspective, the horizontal differences drive the day-to-day search for practices that lead to excellence. And equity is more readily linked to the successful execution of pedagogical practices informed by the conventional instructional cliches. This mismatch creates tensions that, I believe, impede change and create a context for the recycling of deficit theories, research, and pedagogy, a pattern that I examine closely in "Deficit theories, ethnic dialects, and literacy research: When and why recycling is not cost efficient" (Scott, 1992). This treatment of vertical and horizontal differences provides insights into the way that institutional barriers impede changes, and for me this work adds another piece to the deficit recycling puzzle. Through the eyes of teachers, we see more clearly the complexities of trying to practice what we preach about educating for democracy.

Preaching What We Practice

This presentation of views on diversity, literacy, and schools evolves from a teacher-researcher project. Teacher research has become a key mechanism for preaching what we practice. In collaborative work sessions, teacher-researchers preach about what they practice to each other, and, through collaborative writing and publications, teacher-researchers preach what they practice to a wider audience. The value of the approach is not only that it provides a forum for making explicit those implicit understandings that evolve from the wisdom of practice but it also yields results that can be readily applied to schooling problems.

One practical problem to which this work could be applied is that of recruiting and retaining "good" teachers in urban schools where the most diverse of student populations reside. I have often suggested that questions of retention need to be redirected toward why "effective" teachers stay in the urban districts, rather than why they leave. The teachers in this project gave us three basic reasons why they stay: (a) sense of connection with their children and their communities; (b) sense of agency, of ability to make a difference; (c) quality of interaction with colleagues. Embedded in these basic reasons are numerous messages to urban school districts about some of the environmental factors that will likely make a difference in their attracting and retaining a better pool of urban teachers.

In the third reason, quality interactions with colleagues, there is also a message for realizing the professional development goal that was recently added to the America Goals 2000. The value placed on the quality of interaction with colleagues is a recurring theme in discussions of literacy/writing across disciplines, one that has particular relevance to professional development. It is no secret that the fill-the-empty-vessels approach to professional development failed the test of reforming teaching. The message here is that there is a need for more teacher-centered professional development programs. Like students in our classrooms, teachers have needs, knowledge, and experiences that must be taken into consideration in developing professional development or inservice education programs. In their voices, one hears the call for a network of support similar to what teachers provide for students: a setting where they have thinking space, where they can join in the construction of knowledge, where they are respected for their knowledge and experience, and where they can actually preach what they practice as well as benefit from what the expert outsiders preach. In short, we need a constructivist approach to inservice or professional development, and this would be still another way to practice what we preach.

Much of what we know about diversity and education has come from the outside in, from researchers looking at the classroom with preidentified variables and perhaps preconceived notions about what the research should show. The value added by this book is that it provides a look at diversity and differences from the inside. With this has come the explication of particularities about differences, as well as new insights into differences that really make a difference in schools and classrooms. The book says, "Many teachers already practice what the outside experts preach," but it also says, "Many teachers are beginning to preach what the inside experts practice." If ever the two subtexts should meet, life in the urban classroom would become better, for the two would likely converge into a pedagogical stance that views differences and diversity as the norm, as resources that enrich the learning environment, and as means to achieving equity and excellence inside and outside of the school.

Alice Kawazoe continues a dialogic thread found in both Celia Genishi's and Jerrie Cobb Scott's responses: the need for collegial talk. In her own response, Kawazoe points out that people make time for what they value. The experienced teachers whose voices fill this volume make time for children. Do schools make time for them?

Making Time for What We Value
Alice A. Kawazoe
Oakland Unified School District

Despite my deep and abiding faith in good teachers, I could not for the life of me fathom why a small group of them, after a hard day's teaching, would bother to, would care to, would want to trek across town to the university (no matter how tree-shaded the campus), to munch (no matter how good the snacks) and to talk to other teachers every other Tuesday until 7 p.m. or later. The one unit of credit was certainly not the incentive for these veteran teachers. Why would they want to talk about schools and teaching and children instead of going home, eating dinner, having a glass of wine, watching *E.R.* or an update on O.J., gossiping with family or friends, resting, reading a trashy novel, even correcting papers or attending to any of the myriad human activities that move life along?

After reading these chapters capturing the highlights of their time together, I have a partial answer to my question: we do not honor teachers enough to give them any time at school for purposeful conversation, so these teachers must go to the university to talk and to listen, to hear and be heard, to reflect, and to have therapy with "Dr. Dyson." So they carve out time from their personal lives to talk about their teaching lives, and in so doing discover how the threads of care and consternation, fulfillment and frustration, inextricably bind those two lives together.

Teachers lament not having time at school to plan collaboratively. Aside from brief chats in the hallway or during sprints to the bathroom, they apparently have little time ever to talk. But schools make time for what they value: staff meetings, making announcements, perhaps a little professional development, relevant or not, filling out forms, doing needs assessments. If schools do not value planning together, discussing, debating, or researching issues of teaching and learning, or do not trust teachers to use time wisely and well on their own, then no time will be given for these activities. Place can be eliminated easily too. If no one except the principal and the custodian have keys to the kingdom, and the kingdom is locked at 4 p.m. each school day and all weekend, and the drawbridge is raised, then no person—teachers, parents, or children—can cross the moat unless, like Carolyn, they hide out in the dark or sneak in. Schools are locked up; people are locked out.

Carol, one of the participating teachers, asks, "How do you have these kids have a place [in school]?" We can also ask, "How do we have these teachers have a place?" And a truly disturbing question: What does it say of schools if they do not provide time or make a place for children and teachers? We dare not think the answer.

But hope prevails. If schools do not provide time or make a place for the people in them, then these teachers, and others like them, will. In all the discussions of school reform and broad brush change making, we often forget that the smallest, but most significant unit of change is the potentially electric synapse between teacher and child. Carolyn sparks Darian's learning so that he can confidently declare, "You should tell them [the teachers in the group] that at first I didn't get it. . . . Then I got it." Andrea takes the "difficult children," and assures Patsy, the child no one wants, "Yes, Patsy, I like you." Carol asks her second graders how to shape their learning environment to "make it work for them" and worries about Allen. Judy engenders the feeling that "all children are my children" and too, frets that Alberto really is "in danger of losing himself." Jill knows that children "need to have this voice in the classroom."

Phi Long's relatives want Elise to control his video game playing and soup eating, and she does. Louise frets that Faye's verbal skills and excitement will get swallowed by the push to read and gain testable skills. Kristin helps Sammy with his first fearful person-to-person encounter with Chinese American kindergartners. Linda begins a cross-age tutoring program uniting her kindergartners with third- and fourth-grade students. Judi shares with pride a K–6 literary magazine, and knows of

Anita's complex home life from having taught two of her brothers and chatting personally with her father.

Time and again throughout these chapters teachers make connections, joining children with their minds and hearts and with each other. As these teachers explore the issues of difference, we come to know, through the miniportraits they paint, a whole array of children: Tatanka, Patsy, Darian, Faye, Katherine, Dahlia, Alberto, Sammy, Phi Long, James, Eric, Edward, Shane, Rajesh, Ebony, David, Kesha, and a host of other unnamed children whom they touch and change. The teachers help us learn of differences not by discussing categories and definitions or by characterizing groups, but by coming to know in small ways, different individuals. This is not difference writ large, but difference as embodied in individual learners. In short, they put a child's face on difference.

Andrea wonders about teachers who, like ghosts, enter and exit children's lives and asks, "Who am I to them?" We may further ask, "Who are they to us?" In the surge to maintain control in classes and in schools and at the same time to keep students moving along through the grades in groups of 25, 30, 35, or 40 (in secondary schools teachers might be pushing through herds of 150 or more), what happens to the individual gasping for academic oxygen? Well, we all know what happens to humans who are deprived of oxygen: their hearts stop and their brains die. Andrea and other teachers in the group do not want to be ghosts to their students, nor do they want any child to become a phantom to them. They want classrooms abuzz with people, not filled with inanimate objects or featureless masses deprived by inattention to distinction and detail. They make us notice and pay attention to the details of children's behavior and words, the nuances of emotion and attitude. Who are the children to us? Not a mass or herd or conglomerate or amorphous blob, but small, distinctive bundles of energy and promise.

To return to Andrea's question, "Who am I to them?", recently I was in the library of a high school in the early afternoon waiting to see a teacher. I approached a young woman and casually asked her what she was doing in the library. She said she had been kicked out of class and was "hangin' out" in the library until the class period ended. I asked her why she had been kicked out; and, with a shrug of her shoulders as if to say she really didn't care, she conceded that she probably deserved to be kicked out. Then, all of a sudden, her defenses fell, her facade of apathy disappeared, and she declared, "She [the teacher] is such a *mean* person. All I want is someone to care for me." She turned her back to me so that I wouldn't see how upset she was. A few moments went by with me standing dumbly, she collecting herself. She turned, then, and looked me straight in the eyes, and, in a voice half-filled with anguish and half of tears, she cried out softly, "This place hurts my spirit."

Doctors and others can often fix wounded bodies, and sometimes we can mend broken hearts, but it will take powerful healing to soothe hurt spirits. Somehow we know the connection between this young woman's two laments: caring will ease the hurt. I don't think she means caring in a warm, cuddly way. She doesn't want just hugs; she wants some serious attention. She wants someone to care enough for her mind—to teach her, not discard her. She wants someone to care enough for her spirit—to nurture her, not wound her. The slogan for Hallmark cards creeps into mind, "When you care enough to send the very best." As I think of schools and teachers, I want to change the words to, "When you care enough to give the very best." Do we care enough about our young people to give the very best? Finally, as I review the words, thoughts, and efforts of the folks in Anne Dyson's group, I am reassured that these teachers not only care enough, but perhaps care too much, and that they not only give their very best, but they are our very best.

Epilogue

The Permanence of Change and the Power of Reflection

> Life's history is massively contingent—crucially dependent upon odd particulars of history, quite unpredictable and unrepeatable themselves, that divert futures into new channels. . . . We can explain the actual pathways after they unroll, but we could not have predicted their course. And if we could play the game of life again, history would roll down another set of utterly different but equally explainable channels. In this crucial sense, life's history does not work like the stereotype of a high school physics experiment. Irreducible history is folded into the products of time.
>
> **S. J. Gould,** *An Urchin in the Storm: Essays about Books and Ideas*

Although our Tuesday meetings have stopped now, we still get together once in a while. It's always such "good talk," as Elise says. Our casual conversations and occasional meetings reveal the "unpredictable" but "explainable" nature of our professional histories, to use Gould's words. Our pathways, like those of our students, unfold in the interplay of personal agency, social contexts, and the changing demographics, policies, and politics of city schools.

By the time of our first "reunion meeting," six months after the last regular one, eight of the ten teachers in our group had made—or soon would make—a professional change, large or small. For most of us, the changes involved at least some sense of personal possibility. "In just this microcosm of teachers, so many of us have gone on to other [educational] positions," commented Judi; "I think [that's] . . . a reflection of what can happen in the profession," of how varied teachers' professional lives can be. In Louise's words, "All of us, in our professional growth, have said, 'Wait a minute. . . . This has been good for this period of time, and now I need to do this.'"

Louise, for example, had decided to accept a position in a new elementary (K–5) school. Her decision was related to the Berkeley school district's continuing struggles over and with integration (Wagner, 1994a). In the current school configuration, K–3 grade schools, located outside the poorest parts of the city, are integrated; but the 4–6 schools, located inside those city sites, are not integrated because of "white flight" from public to private schools.

The district has decided to reconfigure all its schools into more traditional (K–5) elementary schools. Louise plans to develop a K–1 program in one such flatland school. "In the last thirty years there has not been a K–5 school in that area. . . . I suspect that there will be some neighborhood people who will be thrilled to have a kindergarten finally in a neighborhood that our kids don't have to be bussed to. And the question will be how to attract people from outside the immediate neighborhood into the neighborhood." Louise was facing, she knew, a situation that would be "very difficult and very exciting at the same time."

Elise had already changed positions, but she had less control over her own fate than did Louise. Like many teachers in Chinese bilingual programs, Elise was a fluent speaker of Cantonese but had been unable to pass the difficult written portion of the bilingual credential exam. Indeed, because of just this problem, urban districts, fearful of losing state bilingual funding, hired foreign teachers from abroad without teaching credentials but with the required written skill (Wagner, 1994b). Thus, Elise now found herself in what seemed a surreal situation: she was designated a Vietnamese teacher-in-training at her school; she had five years within which to learn and pass the *Vietnamese* language exam. As Carolyn said, "Somewhere there's a Vietnamese teacher who's teaching Cantonese kids."

Andrea and Linda had changed grade levels and schools. The population of Linda and Andrea's old school was shifting. There were many more Spanish-speaking children and, thus, a need for more bilingual classes. Linda's position was "consolidated out." She had found a position in another flatland school. She liked her new colleagues and delighted in her second graders. But she had thirty-one children cramped into a leaky, 19' X 23' portable building—quarters so cramped that they violated the city fire code.

Andrea, who had begun working on an administrative credential, was, for the first time in her teaching career, at a hills school. Andrea felt appreciated and respected by both parents and fellow teachers in her new position; and she was amazed at the many parents with free time to volunteer at the school and, also, at the school's wealth of equipment. Most importantly, she felt that this school belonged to all of the children and all of the teachers, and she regretted that she had no longer felt that way in her old position:

> You can walk in the supply room. You can use the laminating machine. They have three copy machines. . . . You can go in the book room. You can go in any room in the building. You can walk in the principal's office. People walk in there and use her phone. But the last school I was at, a gate went up saying, "Stop. Unauthorized personnel not allowed." The supply room was closed, and you'd ask the secretary for something, and she'd say, "Well . . . I was told not to let you guys in." So after a while it got very stressful there, to where teachers were beginning to turn on each other because of the frustration.

Judi and Carolyn were both in positions now where they could see the great differences in school circumstance and culture that Andrea mentioned. They had each temporarily left their classrooms and were supervisors in the Beginning Teacher Support and Assessment Program, a state-sponsored pilot project involving local teacher education institutions and the Oakland Public Schools. They were excited by the opportunity to support first-year teachers through advice, materials, and opportunities for "self-assessment," for reflecting on their school experiences and their ways of teaching. "I think," said Carolyn, "we have put out fires where people would have maybe quit." Moreover, they were both inspired by the "pockets of excellence" and the "wonderful teaching going on" at all levels and in all areas of the city.

Judi and Carolyn were providing just the sort of collegiality Kristin had desired the previous year. In search of more support, she too had taken a new job. In her new position, she was primarily responsible for—and had the opportunity to develop—her children's language arts program. She, like Louise, relished the opportunity to develop curricular ideas in what promised to be a supportive, collegial atmosphere.

Jill remained at her old school, but she was planning a temporary leave. Desiring "a change," she accepted a position at the university, helping to disseminate findings from a science education project on which she had worked. Both Judy and Carol also remained at their old schools, and they planned to stay. Each felt they had support and opportunities for growth and, of course, for making a difference in the lives of their students.

For example, during her fifteen years at her school, Carol had been able to teach all grades from kindergarten to fourth (and she hoped to eventually teach fifth), allowing her to experience both children and curriculum across the developmental span of the elementary school. During her eight years at her school, Judy had been involved in many areas of curriculum involvement and, in fact, had just become involved in a mathematics leadership program.

FIGURE 15 | Elise and Kristin talking through our group photo album.

As the meeting progressed, and one teacher after another told of her experiences and plans, the unfolding discussion seemed, to Anne, to return to the opening themes of our first meetings, themes we presented in Chapter 2. Once again, we talked about grade-level designations, language program placements, and race relations, about parent and colleague communication, and, throughout, about the need for balance between teacher agency and possibility and institutional constraint and regulation.

Given the diversity of children in our schools, and the ever shifting sociopolitical circumstances in which we work, opportunities for such reflection seem critical. There can be no rigid prescriptions, no simple lists of activities that "work," no endpoint at which one has "mastered" being a teacher. Good teaching in city schools requires maximum flexibility and creativity, maximum reaching out to children, parents, and colleagues. Moreover, in our view, part of being a good teacher is reaching out to new possibilities for growth— and finding possibilities amidst institutional constraints. One source of such growth is found in opportunities, in Carolyn's words, "to come together . . . and talk about kids."

As educators, our common interest in, appreciation of, and pleasure in knowing children provided a means to explore the complexities of difference, and of the institutional and relational factors that frame those differences as potential problems or resources, as "at risk" indicators or aspects of the normal variation of classroom life. Making such opportunities themselves a normal part of a teacher's life will require widespread changes of institutional organization and epistemological vision. We have offered this document as illustrative evidence of the difference reflection can make, of the strength and support we can collectively offer each other, as we work to make concrete our faith in the future, in our children, and in ourselves.

Works Cited

Bakhtin, M. (1986). *Speech genres and other late essays*. Trans. Vern W. McGee. Austin, TX: University of Texas Press.

Bartolomé, L. (1994). Beyond the methods fetish: Toward a humanizing pedagogy. *Harvard Educational Review, 64,* 173–194.

Cazden, C. (1988). *Classroom discourse: The language of teaching and learning*. Portsmouth, NH: Heinemann.

Cazden, C., & Mehan, H. (1989). Principles from sociology and anthropology: Context, code, classroom, and culture. In M. C. Reynolds (Ed.), *Knowledge base for the beginning teacher* (pp. 47–57). Oxford and New York: Pergamon.

Cochran-Smith, M., & Lytle, S. (1993). *Inside/outside: Teacher research and knowledge*. New York: Teachers College Press.

Cole, J. (1989). *Anna Banana: One hundred one jump-rope rhymes*. New York: Morrow Junior Books.

Comber, B., & O'Brien, J. (1993). Critical literacy: Classroom explorations. *Critical Pedagogy Networker, 6,* 1–11.

Connell, R. W. (1994). Poverty and education. *Harvard Educational Review, 64,* 125–149.

Cortazzi, M. (1993). *Narrative analysis*. London: Falmer.

Darling-Hammond, L. (1993). Reframing the school reform agenda: Developing capacity for school transformation. *Phi Delta Kappan, 74,* 752–761.

Davies, B. (1989). *Frogs and snails and feminist tales: Preschool children and gender*. Boston: Allen & Unwin.

Delpit, L. (1988). The silenced dialogue: Power and pedagogy in educating other people's children. *Harvard Educational Review, 58,* 280–298.

Delpit, L. (1990). Language diversity and learning. In S. Hynds & D. L. Rubin (Eds.), *Perspectives on talk and learning* (pp. 247–266). Urbana, IL: National Council of Teachers of English.

Dyson, A. H. (1993). *Social worlds of children learning to write in an urban primary school.* New York: Teachers College Press.

Enright, D. S. (1986). "Use everything you have to teach English": Providing useful input to young language learners. In *Children and ESL: Integrating perspectives* (pp. 113–162). Washington, DC: Teaching English to Speakers of Other Languages (TESOL).

Erickson, F. (1986). Qualitative methods in research on teaching. In M. C. Wittrock (Ed.), *Handbook of research on teaching* (pp. 119–161). New York: Macmillan.

Erickson, F. (1987). Transformation and school success: The politics and culture of educational achievement. *Anthropology & Education Quarterly, 18,* 335–356.

Fassler, R. Z. (1995). *The role of talk: The growth of the use of English in a self-contained English as a second language urban kindergarten.* Unpublished doctoral dissertation. Teachers College, Columbia, New York.

Florio-Ruane, S. (1989). Social organization of classes and schools. In M. C. Reynolds (Ed.), *Knowledge base for the beginning teacher* (pp. 163–172). Oxford and New York: Pergamon.

Florio-Ruane, S. (1991). Conversation and narrative in collaborative research: An ethnography of the written literacy forum. In C. Witherell & N. Noddings (Eds.), *Stories lives tell: Narrative and dialogue in education* (pp. 234–256). New York: Teachers College Press.

Gag, W. (1977). *Millions of cats.* New York: Coward, McCann & Geoghegan.

Garvey, C. (1990). *Play* (enl. ed.). Cambridge, MA: Harvard University Press.

Genishi, C., Dubetz, N., & Focarino, C. (in press). Reconceptualizing theory through practice: Insights from a first-grade teacher and second language theorists. In S. Reifel (Ed.), *Advances in early education and day care: Vol. 7.* Greenwich, CT: JAI Press.

Genishi, C. (Ed.), (1992). *Ways of assessing children and curriculum: Voices from the classroom.* New York: Teachers College Press.

Gilbert, P. (1994). "And they lived happily ever after": Cultural storylines and the construction of gender. In A. H. Dyson & C. Genishi (Eds.), *The need for story: Cultural diversity in classroom and community* (pp. 124–142). Urbana, IL: National Council of Teachers of English.

Gilmore, P., Goldman, S., McDermott, R., & Smith, D. (1993). Failure's failure. In E. Jacob & C. Jordan (Eds.), *Minority education: Anthropological perspectives* (pp. 209–234). Norwood, NJ: Ablex.

Gould, S. J. (1987). *An urchin in the storm: Essays about books and ideas.* New York: W. W. Norton.

Greene, M. (1988). *The dialectic of freedom.* New York: Teachers College Press.

Guthrie, G. (1992). Bilingual education in a Chinese community: An ethnography in progress. In M. Saravia-Shore & S. F. Arvizu (Eds.), *Cross-cultural literacy: Ethnographies of communication in multiethnic classrooms* (pp. 173–210). New York: Garland.

Gutierrez, K. (1993). Biliteracy and the language-minority child. In O. Saracho & B. Spodek (Eds.), *Yearbook in early childhood education: Vol. 4. Language and literacy in early childhood education* (pp. 82–101). New York: Teachers College Press.

Heath, S. B. (1983). *Ways with words: Language, life and work in communities and classrooms.* Cambridge: Cambridge University Press.

Heilbrun, C. G. (1988). *Writing a woman's life.* New York: Ballantine Books.

Jackson, P. (1990). *Life in classrooms* (reissue). New York: Teachers College Press.

Jacob, E., & Jordan, C. (Eds.). (1993). *Minority education: Anthropological perspectives.* Norwood, NJ: Ablex.

Kingston, M. H. (1976). *The woman warrior: Memoirs of a girlhood among ghosts.* New York: Alfred A. Knopf.

Kunjufu, J. (1984). *Developing discipline and positive self-images in black children.* Chicago: Afro-American Images.

Ladson-Billings, G. (1994). *The dreamkeepers: Successful teachers of African American children.* San Francisco: Jossey-Bass.

Leacock, E. B. (1969). *Teaching and learning in city schools: A comparative study.* New York: Basic Books.

Lensmire, T. (1993). Following the child, socioanalysis, and threats to community: Teacher response to children's texts. *Curriculum Inquiry, 23,* 265–299.

Lightfoot, S. L. (1978). *Worlds apart: Relationships between families and schools.* New York: Basic Books.

Lobel, A. (1970). *Frog and Toad are friends.* New York: Harper & Row.

Martin, J. R. (1992). *The Schoolhome: Rethinking schools for changing families.* Cambridge, MA: Harvard University Press.

McPhail, D. (1989). Boo Bear takes a rest. In *Houghton Mifflin literary readers: Beginning to read* (level C, pp. 45–54). Boston: Houghton Mifflin.

Moll, L., Amanti, C., Neff, D., & Gonzalez, N. (1992). Funds of knowledge for teaching: Using a qualitative approach to connect homes and classrooms. *Theory into Practice, 31,* 132–141.

Montero-Sieburth, M. (1989). Restructuring teachers' knowledge for urban settings. *Journal of Negro Education, 58,* 332–344.

Mora, P. (1992). *A birthday basket for Tia.* New York: Macmillan.

O'Loughlin, M. (1992, September). *Appropriate for whom? A critique of the culture and class bias underlying developmentally appropriate practice in early childhood education.* Paper presented at the Conference on Reconceptualizing Early Childhood Education: Research, Theory, and Practice, Chicago, IL.

Opie, I., & Opie, P. (1959). *The lore and language of schoolchildren.* London: Oxford University Press.

Paley, V. (1986). *Mollie is three: Growing up in school.* Chicago: The University of Chicago Press.

Perry, T., & Fraser, J. (Eds.). (1993). *Freedom's plow: Teaching in a multicultural classroom.* New York: Routledge.

Reyes, M. (1992). Challenging venerable assumptions: Literacy instruction for linguistically different students. *Harvard Educational Review, 62,* 427–446.

Rich, A. (1979). Teaching language in open admissions. In *On lies, secrets, and silence: Selected prose, 1966–1978*. New York: W. W. Norton.

Royster, J., Scott, J. C., & Straker, D. (forthcoming). *Classroom environments: Multidirectional relationships between theory and practice*. Portsmouth, NH: Boynton Cook/Heinemann.

Scott, J. C. (1990). The silent sounds of language variation in the classroom. In S. Hynds & D. Rubin (Eds.), *Perspectives on talk and learning* (pp. 285–297). Urbana, IL: National Council of Teachers of English.

Scott, J. C. (1992). Deficit theories, ethnic dialects, and literacy research: When and why recycling is not cost efficient. In C. Kinzer & D. Leu (Eds.), *Forty-first Yearbook of The National Reading Conference. Literacy research, theory, and practice: Views from many perspectives* (pp. 49–63). Chicago: The National Reading Conference.

Shepard, L. (1991). Negative policies for dealing with diversity: When does assessment and diagnosis turn into sorting and segregation? In E. Hiebert (Ed.), *Literacy for a diverse society: Perspectives, practices, and policies* (279–298). New York: Teachers College Press.

Shulman, L. (1987). Knowledge and teaching: Foundations of the new reform. *Harvard Educational Review, 57,* 1–22.

Sleeter, C. (1993). How white teachers construct race. In C. McCarthy & W. Crichlow (Eds.), *Race, identity, and representation in education* (pp. 157–171). New York: Routledge.

Sleeter, C., & Grant, C. (1987). An analysis of multicultural education in the United States. *Harvard Educational Review, 57,* 421–444.

Smith, A. Deveare. (1993). *Fires in the mirror*. New York: Anchor Books/Doubleday.

Smitherman, G. (1986). *Talkin and testifyin: The language of black America* (rev. ed.). Detroit, MI: Wayne State University Press.

Smitherman, G. (1990). The "mis-education of the Negro"—and you too. In H. A. Daniels (Ed.), *Not only English: Affirming America's multilingual heritage* (pp. 109–120). Urbana, IL: National Council of Teachers of English.

Steedman, C. (1992). *Past tenses: Essays on writing, autobiography, and history.* London: Rivers Oram Press.

Turner, A. W. (1987). *Nettie's trip south.* New York: Macmillan.

Vygotsky, L. S. (1978). *Mind in society: The development of higher psychological processes.* (M. Cole, V. John-Steiner, S. Scribner, & E. Souberman, Eds.). Cambridge, MA: Harvard University Press.

Wagner, V. (1994a, Dec. 11). Integrated schools elude Berkeley. *The San Francisco Sunday Examiner and Chronicle,* pp. C1, C6.

Wagner, V. (1994b, Dec. 19). Bilingual education evolves. *The San Francisco Examiner,* pp. A1, A14.

Williams, P. J. (1991). *The alchemy of race and rights.* Cambridge, MA: Harvard University Press.

Author

Anne Haas Dyson is a former teacher of young children and, currently, professor of language
and literacy in the School of Education at
the University of California at Berkeley. She
studies the social lives and literacy learning
of schoolchildren. Among her publications
are *The Need for Story: Cultural Diversity in
Classroom and Community* (co-edited with
Celia Genishi), *Multiple Worlds of Child Writ-*

ers: Friends Learning to Write, and *Social Worlds of Children Learning to
Write in an Urban Primary School,* which was awarded NCTE's David
Russell Award for Distinguished Research in 1994.

Contributors

Andrea Bennett has been teaching for twenty-three years for the Oakland Unified School District. She is currently a second-grade teacher and mentor at Thornhill School. Her interests include working with the Early Child Developmental Network Group in Oakland.

Wanda Brooks is a graduate student at the University of Pennsylvania. Her research interests include multicultural literature and the historical uses of literacy in African American communities. She has also been a middle school teacher for four years.

Judi Garcia teaches in the Oakland Unified School District, where she has been a primary school teacher for the past twenty-five years. She has taught in many schools and is now a teacher on special assignment with the California Beginning Teacher Support and Assessment Project (BTSA) as well as a teacher consultant for the Bay Area Writing Project. Judi is especially interested in supporting new teachers as they explore writing with their students.

Celia Genishi is professor of education in the Program in Early Childhood Education and Chair of the Department of Curriculum and Teaching at Teachers College, Columbia University. She is a former secondary Spanish and preschool teacher and currently teaches courses related to early childhood education and qualitative research methods. Previously, she was on the faculty at the University of Texas at Austin and Ohio State University. She is co-author (with Anne Haas Dyson) of *Language Assessment in the Early Years;* (with Millie Almy) of *Ways of Studying Children;* editor of *Ways of Assessing Children and Curriculum;* and co-editor (with Anne Haas Dyson) of *The Need for Story: Cultural Diversity in Classroom and Community.* She is also author of many articles about children's language, observation, and assessment. Her research interests include collaborative research on alternative assessment, childhood bilingualism, and language use in classrooms.

Carolyn Howard-McBride is a teacher on special assignment with the Beginning Teacher Support Assessment Project in the Oakland Unified School District. She has taught students from diverse ethnic backgrounds for fourteen years in grades one through four. Her special interests include teacher and student assessment, computer technology, and working with new teachers.

Alice Kawazoe is Director of Curriculum and Staff Development for the Oakland Unified School District, overseeing subject areas from kindergarten through twelfth grade. Previously, as a teacher for twenty-two years, she taught English, ceramics, physical education, and science.

Judy Malekzadeh is a primary school teacher at Melrose School in the Oakland Unified School District. She has been teaching for thirteen years, ten of which have been in a Spanish bilingual classroom. She is currently interested in how children acquire a second language and is researching different methodologies for teaching second-language learners.

Carol Pancho is a teacher at Peralta year-round school where she teaches second and third grade. She has been teaching for seventeen years in kindergarten through fourth-grade classrooms. As a teacher consultant for the Bay Area Writing Project, she has conducted workshops in various school districts, focusing on social studies and literature.

Linda Rogers is a first-grade teacher for the Oakland Unified School District. Ten of her twelve years of teaching were spent in kindergarten. All of her teaching has been in urban schools. She is currently enrolled at the University of California at Berkeley in the Language and Literacy graduate program.

Louise Rosenkrantz is currently a kindergarten teacher in Berkeley, California. A teacher for over twenty-five years, she has taught in a variety of settings including parent cooperative nursery schools and a project for children with parents in prison.

Elizabeth Scarboro has worked in the San Francisco Bay Area and Chicago schools as a teacher and researcher over the past seven years. Her interests include writing and working with diverse student populations. She is the author of two children's books and is currently an elementary school librarian in Cambridge, Massachusetts.

Jerrie Cobb Scott, researcher, educator, and linguist, received her Ph.D. and M.A. in linguistics from the University of Michigan and her B.S. in education from the University of Toledo. Currently Director of the Office of Diversity at the University of Memphis, Scott formerly served as Dean of Education and Director of the Center for Studies of Urban Literacy at Central State University in Wilberforce, Ohio, and Director of Composition at the University of Florida in Gainesville. Her areas of research and publication are diversity, language variation, multicultural education, and literacy. Her professional services include being a member of the Advisory Board of the Center for the Study of Writing and Literacy at the University of California, Berkeley, founder and national director of the African American Read-In Chain, and member of the NCTE Editorial Board.

Kristin Stringfield has spent the past nine years teaching children from various ethnic and socioeconomic backgrounds throughout California. She enjoys teaching writing and has worked with both the University of California at Irvine Writing Project and the Bay Area Writing Project. Kristen is currently a fourth-grade teacher at the East Bay Sierra School in El Cerrito, California.

Jill Walker is currently teaching first grade in the Oakland Unified School District. She has been teaching for twenty years, including first through fourth grade as well as deaf and hearing-impaired students of all ages.

Elise Yee is a kindergarten teacher for the Oakland Unified School District. She enjoys this age group because every day presents a new challenge. Throughout her thirty-five years of teaching, Elise has found that working with children can be fun and exciting.

———

*This book was typeset in Bembo, Mrs. Eaves, and Eurocrat,
and the typeface used on the cover was Eurocrat.
The paper was 50 lb. Finch.*

than good. Louise and Kristin mentioned the importance of allotting plenty of time, including weekends, for such activities, so that they did not add to the daily stresses of home life. And Elise and Carolyn pointed out that home activities could potentially highlight parents' own difficulties with literacy in English or in their home language.

The mother of Darian, Carolyn's focal child, reported how angry her son had been with her when she had been unable to help him complete a robot-building project. "My interpretation of that," said Carolyn, "is that when [homework] requires adult assistance or requires materials that may not be right at hand, [which] she has to give to him or assist him with, that that takes up too much time because she doesn't have that kind of time." An oral "interview," requiring only key words on a form (like names of candies and games), was much more likely to be done at home—and to yield rich conversations and literacy activities in school.

In addition to the family strains indirectly revealed through our activities, we also found ourselves responding more directly to complex issues raised by the children themselves. For example, when Carol's class constructed comparative charts on the cities of Oakland and Oakley, the children raised issues of community violence; when Wanda asked Edward, who did not identify with pinatas and birthday dances, about his own community ways, he worried about his big brother's way of dressing and about how people might assume he was in a gang; and when Kristin's children prepared for their trip to Chinatown, children's perceptions (and misperceptions) of local ethnic communities (including why, or even if, people choose to live together) came to the fore.

We had no answers to offer the children, but talking through issues—listening to each child's perspective, comparing those perspectives, clarifying the children's confusions, supplying needed information—could be an answer in and of itself, as Jill suggested in another story about her focal child, Shane:

Jill: I realize that before they can even write [about important matters] they need to have this voice in the classroom. . . . Since reconfiguration in November . . . everybody started talking and feeling comfortable. They know that they're not going to be put down for what they say, because what they say is important. Someone else can feed off of that. . . . Today we were reading a story about Harriet Tubman, and it talked about how she was punished for making mistakes. And [Shane], who lived on the street with a younger sibling for about six months, raised his hand and said, "But we don't get punished for making mistakes. Things have changed." I was blown away, and I said, "Yes things have changed." He said, "We always try to talk things out." All of it came right there, and everybody agreed.

Complaining Memos, Teasing Stories, and Other Ways of Writing Relationships

A classroom, like any other singular group of people, contains a complex of dynamic, interpersonal relationships. Every day there are moments of disagreement and irritation, of giggles and good laughs, of good-hearted generosity and forced sharing. In our classrooms, the medium of writing could serve as an important tool for both revealing the nature of, and helping to negotiate, relationships among teachers and children, *and* that negotiating in turn can support the development of writing itself.

Carolyn: Last week I just got so tired with tattling that I have to tell you about this.

Judi: Oh, I know.

Carolyn: I couldn't take it. . . . So I got one of those bins from Safeway, that they have the dried foods in, . . . I said, "This is my mail box. If you have a problem that is not serious [enough] that I need to stop teaching, but it is something you want me to deal with, write me a note and put it in there. I thought, "Never. They will never write me a note." . . . It was amazing to me the language that kids used!. . . This one is written like a memo, "To Mrs. McBride. I want my seat to be changed because Vandell talks to me on the rug. From Edward.". . . This is from Edward,

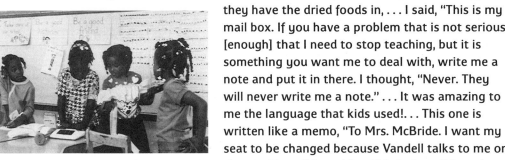

FIGURE 10 | Taking a message in Linda's room.

"Julio laughed at me when Ms._____ grabbed me for no reason."
Ms.____ is [a volunteer]. She shouldn't have been grabbing him at
all. That helped me to see the relationship. . . . I learned so much
about things that irritated them, and where they got upset. It
really pushed their writing. . . .

Andrea: I have something like you do. I had a form in first grade and
surprisingly they could fill it out. In upper grades, I have who,
when, where, and what happened. Then it says, "I have a problem." Then hanging at the bottom of my table it says, "Drop your
problems here." Lately I've noticed that there were stacks, but on
there it says, "Do you need the teacher's help?" They will put *no*
and give it to me anyway.

Louise: I think that is wonderful.

Judi: I am going to start this.

Louise: The putting of "no" validates that you know about the problem,
but that you don't have to do anything. . . .

Carol: [commenting on her children's letters, written on Fridays, about
how class is going for them] . . . It just gives me a sense of problems that come up that I don't grasp in the general classroom . . .
and it's easier for me to respond in that way to them as well. I find
to respond to journal entries is difficult for me. "That's great. You
have a dog? I have one too." It seems so trite.

In our discussions, then, we linked social knowledge, literate
know-how, and problem solving. Our reports on individual children contained many examples of children exploiting (and pushing) their understanding of literacy genres so that they could manipulate the social world,
particularly each other, in some way. To illustrate, in Judy's school, children wrote directly to each other when they had problems to resolve.
The official form letter began "Dear_____." But Judy's focal child,
Alberto, who struggled with writing, crossed out "Dear" in his letter to
a tattle-telling peer: he understood something of how to violate literacy
conventions in order to express his feelings to the offending other.

Carol told about how her children had started using written
stories in similar ways. Her third graders used "each other's names and

changing stories around" both to play with each other—and to irritate each other "after they'd gotten into fights on the playground." The children understood the social situation and story conventions, and they knew how to manipulate those stories to "please" or to "get" people, if need be. (They did need to learn, as Carol pointed out, about seeking permission before including another's name in a public text.)

For some children, the intertwining of peer relationships and literacy use was critically important for their own learning, as Kristin noted when she compared her own focal child, Sammy, with Judy's Dahlia. Dahlia was very oriented to engaging in teacher-assigned school activities, and she placed much value on school markers of achievement. Judy reported how pleased six-year-old Dahlia was when asked to meet with the "experienced writers" (mainly seven-year-olds) who were going to study periods. Kristin, on the other hand, felt Sammy was very differently oriented:

Kristin: I was thinking that while you were talking [Judy], how different Sammy is. . . . [Sammy seemed to put little evident value on pleasing Kristin as teacher.] He really has a desire to belong [in the peer group]. . . . And the thing that happened with Sammy is that when I do writing workshop, I have Author's Theater, and the author gets to choose who's going to be in the play of their story. . . . And then [the authors] read their story, and the people act it out. . . . He usually will do X-men, Ninja Turtles, Three Ninjas, and started doing Power Rangers this year. And everybody suddenly wants to be in Sammy's play. They want his attention. . . . So Sammy suddenly became a writer when he realized the power he had with his peers. . . . Sammy, like I said, was barely writing anything before and now he's getting a lot of things out.

This intertwining of children's lives as peers and literacy users also revealed social issues needing classroom discussion and reflection. For example, in Sammy's second-grade superhero stories, as in those in many other boys' superhero stories, only middle-class white girls were picked for the "female victim" roles and, moreover, there were very few superhero roles for girls—an issue raised by several of the girls in Kristin's